Educating the HEART

Standards-Based Activities to Foster Character, Community, and Self-Reflection

ALISON HAGEE

Zephyr Press

Tucson, Arizona

Educating the Heart
Standards-Based Activities to Foster Character, Community, and Self-Reflection

Grades K–8

© 2003 by Alison Hagee
Printed in the United States of America

ISBN: 1-56976-149-3

Editing: Melanie Mallon
Design and Production: Dan Miedaner
Cover: Dan Miedaner
Photographs and Illustrations: Alison Hagee

Published by:
Zephyr Press
P.O. Box 66006
Tucson, Arizona 85728-6006
800-232-2187
www.zephyrpress.com
www.i-homeschool.com

All rights reserved. The purchase of this book entitles the individual teacher to reproduce some activity sheets for use in the classroom. The reproduction of any part for an entire school or school system or for commercial use is strictly prohibited. No form of this work may be reproduced, transmitted, or recorded without written permission from the publisher. Requests for such permissions should be addressed to Zephyr Press. The Internet is an open and rapidly changing system; websites may contain material inappropriate for children. Educational best practice indicates that an adult should preview all websites before sending students to visit them.

 Zephyr Press is a registered trademark of Zephyr Press, Inc.

Library of Congress Cataloging-in-Publication Data

Hagee, Alison, 1966-
    Educating the heart : standards-based activities to foster character, community, and self-reflection / Alison Hagee.
        p. cm.
    Includes bibliographical references and index.
    ISBN 1-56976-149-3 (alk. paper)
    1. Moral education. 2. Character—Study and teaching—Activity programs. 3. Spiritual life—Study and teaching—Activity programs. I. Title.

LC268 .H22 2002
370.11'4--dc21   2002024545

The following people, schools, and organizations have generously given permission to adapt their activities for this edition:

Buddy Reading, p. 5, and Multiple Intelligences, p. 90, adapted from activities by Denise LaRoque, Pathfinder School, Seattle School District

Life Circle, p. 16, Gleaning, p. 46, and All about Me, p. 78, adapted from activities by Denise LaRoque and Lisa DeBurle, Pathfinder School, Seattle School District

Rotating Art, p. 34, Positive Thoughts, p. 68, and Character, p. 108, adapted from activities by Jill Duff, Pathfinder School, Seattle School District

Me Puzzle, p. 36, adapted from an activity by Lisa Rauch, Madrona School, Seattle School District

America's First People, p. 60, adapted from an activity posted on www.carolhurst.com (Carol Hurst's Children's Literature Site), Copyright 1999, Carol Hurst and Rebecca Otis

Kindness Tree, p. 64, and Word Tools, p. 74, adapted from activities by Maria Callahan, Pathfinder School, Seattle School District

Talking Circle, p. 70, and Clan Animal, p. 116, adapted from activities by Pathfinder School, Seattle School District

Trust Walk, p. 72, and My Culture, p. 98, adapted from activities by Willard Bill, Jr., Pathfinder School, Seattle School District

Acknowledgments

I would like to thank the teachers and staff of Pathfinder School in the Seattle School District, and especially Denise LaRoque, Jill Duff, Lisa DeBurle, Maria Callahan, and Willard Bill, Jr., for their wonderful activity ideas and for the work they do in the classroom. Many of the activities included in this guide are based on their ideas. (See the copyright page for specific credits.) I would also like to thank the children of Pathfinder School, especially the Otter Clan of 1999, who have taught me endless lessons about teaching, the importance of laughter, and unconditional love.

On a personal note, I would like to thank my master's project advisor, Micki Evans, for guiding me in the book-writing process. I would also like to thank my family and friends for their support and love, especially my mom for recognizing and nurturing the whole child in me, letting me make my own mistakes, and guiding me with her gentle wisdom. A special thank you to my life partner and best friend, Eric, for loving me through the best and worst of times and for reminding me to take life a little less seriously. It's supposed to be fun!

From l–r: Denise LaRoque, Jill Duff, Lisa DeBurle, Maria Callahan, and Willard Bill, Jr.

Contents _____

Preface

Children are our gifts. They come to this world with open hearts and soaring spirits. They invite each new experience with curiosity, approach each being they see with kindness in their eyes, and laugh out loud at simple pleasures. As families, teachers, and communities, we hold their futures in our hands. It is an awesome responsibility.

> Our popular culture celebrates the material and largely ignores the spiritual. Greed is the order of the day. We have become a numbers-oriented culture that puts more faith in what we can see, touch, and hear, and are suspicious of the unquantifiable, the intuitive, the mysterious. (Lear 1991, 33)

I believe that our role as teachers is to educate not only the mind but also the heart. We begin to counteract some of the violence, materialism, and competition children are exposed to on a daily basis by using the principles of holistic education, as described by Ron Miller (2000), and by integrating curriculum with activities that educate the heart, supporting the inner lives of children and helping them understand and relish their connections with the world.

From personal experience, I know that attention to the heart is essential to a fulfilling life. I am happier and more at peace with the world and my place in it when I stay connected to myself and what is truly important to me. Children in classrooms that support the development of heart—the search for meaning and purpose in our lives and in our relationships—will find activities and places that make them happier, more peaceful, and more accepting of themselves. They will begin to realize that they feel at peace when they are in nature, writing in a journal, listening to soft music, dancing, creating with their hands, sitting in silence, playing with their friends, or any of the countless ways people find to reconnect to what is important to them.

Principles of Holistic Education

1. Human beings are complex creatures, composed of many layers: biological, ecological, psychological, and emotional dimensions around a spiritual core. As many-layered people, we interact in ideological as well as social and cultural environments.

2. Human development is both personal *and* universal (or spiritual).

3. The spirituality innate in all humans is not purely mystical. It exists within our social and cultural realities.

4. Holistic education is about developing meaningful relationships within a learning community, and therefore it cannot be encapsulated in a technique or set of techniques.

Who Am I? Who Do I Want to Be?

It is often helpful for people of all ages to consider these life questions many times and to redefine themselves with the answers they find. This guidebook is designed to provide students with opportunities throughout the school year to ponder their questions and to learn and grow with their answers.

Much of the violence, anger, fear, and sadness we see in children today stems from neglecting their inner lives and from their disconnection from self, community, and nature. As we educate the heart, we have a unique opportunity to create an environment that nurtures the whole child, to reach all children, and, perhaps, to make a change in a positive direction for humanity, the Earth, and all its creatures.

—Alison Hagee

Introduction

The idea of educating the heart, or spirit, in public schools is not a new concept. In the early twentieth century, Rudolf Steiner created Waldorf schools, and Maria Montessori started the Montessori schools. Both of these schools are based on the spiritual unfolding in child development, on the idea that only when we create learning environments that honor and allow this aspect of a child to develop do we teach the whole child.

Abraham Maslow (1971), cofounder of humanistic psychology, developed new language to describe his model of human development, which included the idea of self-actualization as a human need. *Self-actualization* involves

"experiencing fully, vividly, selflessly, with full concentration and total absorption" (45). It involves finding out one's likes, dislikes, and life mission, and listening to one's inner voice. Maslow incorporates these ideas into his view on education:

> Ultimately the best way of teaching, whether the subject is mathematics, history, or philosophy, is to make the students aware of the beauties involved. We need to teach our children unitive perception, the Zen experience of being able to see the temporal and the eternal simultaneously, the sacred and the profane in the same object. (191)

Ron Miller (1999) notes that several thinkers support the view that "the purpose of education, indeed of human existence itself, is not individual success but the evolution of consciousness" (22). Among these thinkers are Maria Montessori, Rudolf Steiner, Parker Palmer, Jiddu Krishnamurti, Alfred N. Whitehead, Martin Luther King, Jr., Abraham Joshua Heschel, and Ken Wilber.

Ken Wilber has developed a comprehensive and integrated holistic theory by drawing on insights from an incredible variety of these sources (including Whitehead's cosmology). His conclusions explicitly support the mystics' and theologians' claims that the ultimate purpose of human existence is to further the evolution of spirit. (25)

Miller suggests that educators recognize and honor this evolution rather than continue to treat economic success as the highest goal for humanity.

The cognitive, social, emotional, physical, and aesthetic lines of human development have been in the language of educators and the general public for many years, some for longer than others. Theorists on human development have acknowledged spiritual development for almost as long as other lines of development, yet schools tend to shy away from supporting this important dimension of children.

My hope is that we as educators will begin to recognize not only the necessity of supporting this inner core of children but also the exciting possibilities involved in educating the heart.

Children spend much of their young lives at school. The classroom could be a place that allows them to ask and answer their own questions and that encourages growth in all aspects of development.

Guiding Concepts

As educator Aostre N. Johnson (1999) has discovered, many educators want to contribute to their students' spiritual education but feel they can't because they teach in a public school. Several years ago, Johnson began to research the question: In what ways is spirituality currently understood and practiced in relation to education? Through her study of literature and her discussions with more than 80 educators, she has uncovered at least eight different approaches to spirituality in education: objective study of religion, meaning

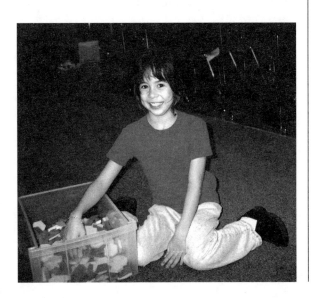

making, self-reflection, mystical knowing, emotion, morality, ecology, and creativity. These eight approaches emphasize the diverse ways in which spirituality is defined.

Johnson recognizes the complexities that educating spirit introduces; however, she insists that to "exclude spiritual perspectives because they are controversial is neither a democratic nor a postmodern solution" (48). She further believes that "all educators who are helping their students to find significant connections in their lives are educators of spirit, each in their own way" (48).

I have used Johnson's research findings as guiding concepts for selecting and developing activities to include in this guide. I have modified three concepts to better fit into public school guidelines and added one based on my own research of how people define spirituality. These guiding concepts are detailed below.

Meaning making

We seek the meaning and purpose of life by asking and searching for answers to questions about ourselves, the world around us, and the nature of life. These are the questions that humans have been asking throughout history and across cultures. This tendency to seek meaning and purpose distinguishes us from other species on Earth. Meaning is often found through relationships with other people and with nature. This seeking is a lifelong pursuit and can begin at an early age if children are given the opportunity and encouragement to do so.

Creativity

When we tap into our creativity, we tap into the core of our being. Creativity flows from the deepest truth of who we are, which often gets lost in the hustle and bustle of everyday life. If children are encouraged to find their unique creative gifts and to make time to connect with them, they will stay connected to their inner selves throughout their lives. It's also important to understand that we *create* our own lives through the decisions we make and the way we choose to approach situations.

Intuitive knowing

Intuition is the ability we all have to access intelligence that isn't quantifiable or visible. Many of us are so influenced by external messages and pressures that we stop listening to and trusting our own intuition (our thoughts, inner voices, and gut feelings). Intuition has been defined as instinct, as God, as our soul, and as our true self, among other things. Whatever the definition, those who learn to trust their intuition make better decisions for themselves and lead more fulfilling lives as a result.

Connections

We learn about ourselves through our interactions with the world around us—through relationships with family and friends, nature, art, music, a higher power (for some), and so forth. Through these interactions, we experience what it is to be human. We experience love, pain, joy, suffering, and everything in between. Part of being a fulfilled person is experiencing life and learning and growing from those experiences. We can help children with this learning and growth by creating situations in which they can make connections with their world.

Character

Regardless of a person's culture, religion, or upbringing, there are universal beliefs about what constitutes good character, such as honesty, kindness, and generosity. We share certain ideas about how human beings should relate to each other. The earlier children begin to understand that we should treat other people the way we want to be treated, the more they will incorporate that behavior into their lives. Children must, therefore, examine how they would like to be treated, how they define right and wrong, and what it means to be a good person.

Self-reflection

Self-reflection is the ability to look deeply into ourselves, to understand our beliefs, emotions, desires, and so forth. It allows us the opportunity to hear our inner voices. Through self-reflection, children can discover their own life purposes (for instance, what careers would be most fulfilling to them) and they can find answers to difficult life questions. The more children understand themselves, the more they will understand others and the world itself.

Emotion

Emotions can tell us much about ourselves and guide us to more fulfilling lives. By experiencing and evaluating our emotions, we can discover what is important to us and make better decisions for ourselves. Many people have been taught to ignore or bury their feelings, which can result in anxiety, misplaced anger, physical problems, poor choices, a disconnection from self, and so forth. Children can learn how to pay attention and understand their emotions and what causes them. They can learn when and how to experience emotions in a healthy way and how to make good choices for themselves based on their emotions.

Nature

Everything in the universe is interconnected. When we do harm to part of our world, we do harm to ourselves. By observing and learning about nature, children will begin to understand this important relationship. By immersing themselves in nature, children will begin to

appreciate the beauty and interconnectedness of the system they are part of, and they will then have a desire to protect it in the future. Being in nature can be calming and soothing or it can be exciting and awe inspiring—all of which nourish our inner cores.

Religion (objective study)

Religion is intertwined with all aspects of life-history, culture, tradition, family life, art, and music, among others. It is therefore impossible to teach about these areas without also exposing children to religion. Many people of the world seek spirituality through one of many organized religions, and many religions have similar beliefs, such as a version of the Golden Rule (that is, treat others as you wish to be treated). Learning about other religions can help children understand other people, see other perspectives, and respect the differences as well as recognize the similarities among people of the world.

Questions and Answers Related to Teaching to the Spiritual Side of Children

The very word "spirituality" is controversial in the context of our public schools, but should it be?

Isn't it against the law to teach spirituality?

It is against the law to teach a specific religion, but spirituality is not synonymous with religion. Religions were developed to try to answer the questions of spirituality: Who am I? Why am I here? What is the meaning of life? It is within the law to teach about different religions (objectively) just as one might teach about different cultures. This book is not about teaching a particular belief system, but rather about giving children the opportunity to find their own way, to connect to their own spiritual paths.

Religion doesn't belong in public schools.

Objective study of religion does belong in public schools just as objective study of history and culture belongs. One cannot learn truth about the world without learning about the religions of the world. Religion is an integral part of humanity. It is against the law to support and teach a particular religion in public schools. This law is important because it respects children of all beliefs. But again, spirituality is not religion. All religions are attempting to answer the questions of spirituality, questions all humans share, regardless of our beliefs. It is not the goal of this book to give children the answers to their spiritual questions but to encourage them to ask the questions so they can find their own answers.

Isn't "spirituality" just a new-age religion?

The so-called "new age" religions attempt to answer spiritual questions with a specific belief system and set of answers just as any other religion does. Spirituality, as used in this book, is not a set of answers and is not synonymous

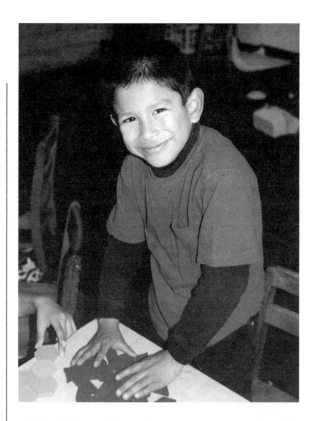

with religion. Spirituality involves seeking truth, which we must find on our own. This book attempts to create situations and experiences through which children can explore their spiritual questions.

How can we teach to the spiritual side of children and still meet academic standards?

Almost all of the activities in this book meet one or more of the academic standards while also educating the heart. Any academic activity that encourages creativity, critical thinking, relationships with others, or self-reflection will also support the spiritual dimension of children.

Spirituality means so many different things to different people. Is it even possible to teach it without impressing my beliefs on the children?

This book does not endorse *teaching* spirituality or a specific set of beliefs. Rather, the point of this book is to emphasize that support for the spiritual development of children is as important as supporting every other aspect of development. For instance, there are many ways to support a child's physical development (physical education class, drama, dance, yoga, recess), and each child will find that one or two of these ways works better for him or her than the others do. This book details activities that support children's spiritual development, enabling them to find out for themselves which work best. Even if a teacher prefers yoga to kick ball, he or she will provide opportunities for children to try both and then let them decide which they like better. In the same manner, this book includes activities that expose children to many different ideas and ways of thinking and believing, and then encourages children to choose what works best for them.

Teaching spirituality is the parents' job, not the school's.

Teaching a specific religion or set of beliefs *is* a parent's job. This book is not about teaching spirituality but about teaching to the heart. It's about creating opportunities for spiritual development, which includes seeking meaning, understanding and listening to one's own thoughts and feelings, finding strengths, defining right and wrong, and so forth. For many children, their spiritual development is supported at home through the study of a particular religion. But many more are never given the opportunity or encouragement to develop spiritually and, therefore, they have difficulty in adulthood. The activities in this book will only enhance whatever is being taught at home.

How is this going to prepare our children for the real world?

In the real world, people need to be able to relate to, and respect, people from all walks of life (different cultures, religions, and so forth). They need to understand and express their emotions in a healthy manner. It's to their advantage to learn how to pursue a life path that is fulfilling and that makes them happy. They will understand that the Earth and its people must be treated with respect (an issue that is of great importance at this time in our history). All of these issues as well as many others are addressed by the activities in this book.

Using This Guide

This activity guide is a collection of stand-alone activities, thematic units (with connected activities), and yearlong themes (with connected units) that teach to the heart of children.

Activities

The stand-alone activities in chapters 1 through 6 are organized by subject:

- reading and writing (chapter 1)
- science and math (chapter 2)
- art and music (chapter 3)
- physical (chapter 4)
- social studies (chapter 5)
- community and connections (chapter 6)

You can easily incorporate these activities into an existing curriculum. Because it is important to create a safe environment for children to explore their spiritual dimensions, you may want to begin with the activities in the community and connections chapter. See the box at right for a list of activity components.

Activity Format

Each activity in chapters 1 through 6 begins with a sidebar that lists

- the learning standards each activity addresses (see pages 122–23 for definitions of these standards)
- the guiding concepts for each activity (see pages viii–x for definitions of these categories)
- the multiple intelligences each activity uses (see page 124 for definitions of the multiple intelligences)

After the sidebar, each activity includes the following components:

- **Goals:** This section lists the main objectives of the activity, such as what students will learn and accomplish.
- **Time:** This section includes an estimate of how long the activity will take (in minutes, hours, or days). Note that this may vary depending on the size of your class and whether you adapt or vary the activity.
- **Grade Range:** Here you will find the range of grades for which the activity is most appropriate. Note that the Variations section often includes ideas for adapting the activity to suit older or younger students, from kindergarten through eighth grade.
- **Materials:** This section lists all supplies (such as art materials, books, paper, pencils) you and your students will need to complete the activity.
- **Setup:** In this section, you'll find any preparatory steps you need to take before introducing the activity to your students.
- **Instructional Sequence:** This section describes the activity itself, broken down into sequential steps.
- **Assessment:** Here you'll find assessment questions to ask yourself as you observe and evaluate student progress before, during, and after the activity.
- **Variations:** This section includes ideas for varying the activity to suit different student needs and ages or simply to add variety.

Thematic Units

Chapter 7 includes several activities that explore the same themes, grouped together into thematic units:

- All about Me
- Multiple Intelligences
- My Culture

Each unit begins with an About This Unit section that lists the activities in the unit, including a time estimate for each activity. The first pages of the unit include sections similar to those found in the stand-alone activities (as described in the box opposite):

- Goals
- Time (to complete all activities in the unit)
- Grade Range
- Assessment (for the unit as a whole)
- Variations (to the unit as a whole)

Each activity page in the unit includes Materials, Setup, Instructional Sequence, Assessment, and Variations sections with information that pertains to that specific activity.

Yearlong Themes

Chapter 8 includes two yearlong themes—learning adventures that thematically tie together several activities and projects throughout a school year:

- Character
- Clan Animals

Each of these yearlong themes is an outline of ideas and resources for an in-depth learning experience for children. The first pages of each theme describe the unit(s), goals, grade range, assessment, and variations for that particular theme. These introductory pages also include a list of resources (such as books and videos) you may find useful as you and your students embark on a yearlong theme.

Subsequent pages list activity and project ideas, grouped by the units each theme comprises if applicable. For example, Character includes four units: Respect, Generosity, Courage, and Pride. Each unit includes a list of activity and project ideas that focus on the unit topic, plus ideas for assessment for that particular unit. Clan Animal is one long, extended unit, with activities and projects you can implement throughout the year, plus assessment ideas for particular activities and projects.

Your children are not your children. They are the sons and daughters of life's longing for itself.

—Kahlil Gibran

Appendices

Three appendices include further information and resources to help you get the most out of the activities in this book.

- Appendix A: Standards and Multiple Intelligences includes information about learning standards and multiple intelligences, which both inform this book.

- Appendix B: Worksheets for Activities contains worksheets you can photocopy for your students to use with particular activities.

- Appendix C: Resources and References lists a wide range of books, videos, music, and websites for you and your students to use with the activities, units, and themes in this book. The resources are organized by activity and by subject category, with an additional section of resources just for teachers interested in more information on supporting the spiritual side of children. The references that inform this book are listed in a separate section at the end.

Chapter 1

Reading and Writing Activities

Creation Stories _____

Guiding Concepts
(See pages viii–x.)
- Meaning making
- Religion (objective study)
- Creativity
- Connections
- Self-reflection

Multiple Intelligences
(See page 124.)
- Verbal-linguistic
- Visual-spatial
- Intrapersonal

Goals

- Students will learn about different cultures, understand that there are many different ways to live and think, and appreciate diversity.
- Students will demonstrate and identify with what they've learned from the creation stories of other cultures by writing their own creation stories.

Time

30 minutes a day for several days to read each story; 3 hours to create stories

Grade Range

2–8

Materials

- ✔ several creation stories from different cultures
- ✔ globe or world atlas
- ✔ pens, crayons, or pastels
- ✔ computer with printer and paper or several sheets of paper

Setup

Find several creation stories from different cultures: about the origin of the Earth, people, and so forth. (See page 141 for some ideas.) If you teach students who are just learning to write, be sure to pick stories that include pictures.

Instructional Sequence

1. Show the cover of a creation story. Explain to students that you will be reading some stories from different parts of the world during the next several days. Students should think about how the stories are the same and how they are different.

2. Introduce the first story: Read the title and describe or name the culture from which the story is derived.

3. Show on the globe or in the atlas where the culture is (or was).

4. Read the story.

5. Ask students how this type of story is different from other stories you have read in class. Explain to students that creation stories are written to explain the world. They are sometimes based on fact and are often handed down through generations.

6. Ask students what ideas they have about the story you just read: "What is the story about? Does the story have lessons? What aspect of the world or of life does the story explain? What questions does the story answer (such as How did the Earth begin and why are there stars)?" Start a list of the lessons, explanations, and answered questions found in the story.

7. After you have read a few more stories to the class and have discussed each story's lessons, explanations, and answered questions, discuss the elements of creation stories. Ask students: "What are the common elements among these stories?" Start a list of elements. For example, are there character types common to each story (such as heros, wise people or animals, villains)? Do the stories share a similar setting (including time as well as place)? Do any of the stories attempt to explain the same thing, such as the same aspect of how the world came to be, or the same lesson?

8. After you have read all the stories, tell students they will write their own creation stories. They can work in small groups or by themselves. Their creation stories should answer some question about the world. It may or may not include a lesson, but it should have some interesting characters and some of the elements the class found in the creation stories you read.

9. Students should start with rough drafts, which they will edit and then type on computers (if possible). They can illustrate their stories as well. Younger students who are just learning to write might include fewer words (or no words) and more drawings.

Assessment

As you read and discuss the creation stories, consider the following:

- Do students listen to and comprehend the creation stories?

- Do students participate in whole group discussions (by either listening actively or adding their own ideas)?

- Are students respectful of other cultures' creation stories and beliefs?

Evaluate students' own creation stories with the following questions in mind:

- Do students include elements of a creation story in their own stories?

- Do students use the writing process (prewriting, drafting, revising, editing, publishing)?

- How well do students incorporate the writing traits (ideas, organization, voice, word choice, sentence fluency, conventions, presentation) as appropriate for their age group?

- Do students put care and effort into their illustrations?

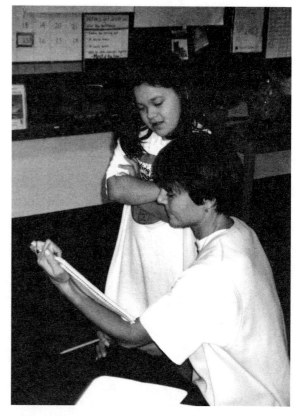

"What else could you say here?"

Prejudice is the child of ignorance.

—William Hazlitt

Variations

- Students could write a creation story as a class instead of as individuals.

- Students could share their creation stories with the class.

- Students could write a creation story as a skit in small groups. Groups then take turns performing their stories.

- Students could choose two of the stories you read in class and write papers to compare and contrast them.

- You could discuss with the class the oral traditions of some cultures who pass on their creation stories through storytellers. (If possible, invite a storyteller to visit your class and share a tale.)

A student wonders how the sky was created.

Buddy Reading

Standards
(See pages 122–23.)

- Reading
- Communication

Guiding Concepts
(See pages viii–x.)

- Meaning making
- Character
- Connections

Multiple Intelligences
(See page 124.)

- Verbal-linguistic
- Interpersonal

Goals

- Students will help younger students develop reading fluency, strategies for reading unfamiliar words (sounding out, using context, using pictures), and comprehension skills.

- Students will build self-esteem, responsibility, and interpersonal skills by playing the role of the big kid and teacher.

- Students will make connections with other people.

Time

20–30 minutes per week during the entire year

Grade Range

3–8

Materials

- ✔ several books in the classroom and school library to suit the range of reading levels in the younger class (such as *Obo,* by B. Anderson, and *All I See Is Part of Me,* by C. M. Curtis)

Setup

Find a teacher of a lower grade whose class would be willing to participate in buddy reading with your class. Set up a time for the two classes to spend 20 to 30 minutes together once a week.

Building community—third graders read to a kindergarten student.

Instructional Sequence

1. Ask the older students: "Have you ever been the teacher?" Discuss student responses, allowing time for students to share stories about teaching and their definitions of what teaching is.

2. Ask students if they can remember what strategies they learned when they first started reading. Guide the discussion to cover strategies such as sounding out words, getting clues from pictures, recognizing words on sight, and reading comprehension strategies, such as figuring out words from context.

3. Explain to the students that they will each pair up with a buddy reader, a younger student who will read aloud with them. The younger readers get to choose what books they will read.

4. Remind students that they are the big kids and should be role models for the little kids. They should speak in quiet voices and be responsible about staying on task. They should try to teach reading strategies (as discussed in step 2) to their buddies.

5. Split students between two classrooms and help older students pair up with younger reading buddies (the pairs will be the same throughout the year).

6. Older students help the younger students choose books and a quiet place for reading. Older students are responsible for keeping their reading buddies focused.

7. After the first reading session, older students return to class to discuss how things went. Discussion could include ways to improve the experience, general questions and concerns about the experience, and suggestions for how to help the younger students even further. Throughout the year, hold follow-up discussions as needed to keep students on track and to help them help their buddies as much as possible.

Assessment

During and after each experience, evaluate how well students work with their reading buddies:

- Do students respect their reading buddies' choices?

- Are students patient while younger students read?

- Do students stay on task?

- Do students help their reading buddies use strategies to read unfamiliar words, such as sounding them out, using context, and using pictures?

- Do students talk with their buddies about the stories to gauge and help develop comprehension skills?

Variations

- If you teach young students, you could initiate this activity with an older class. The instructional sequence might include helping the younger children select books and discussing how the older students will be helping them. The younger students would enjoy knowing some of the older kids around school.

- Students could take turns reading during each session, so the older students model reading skills (such as inflection and pronunciation) and the younger students get a break from nonstop reading.

- If class sizes don't match up, you could try this activity in groups of three, with two older kids and one younger, or two younger kids and one older.

- Both older and younger students could choose books to read, taking turns reading their selections each session.

- For extra credit, older students could develop techniques, such as vocabulary flash cards, to help their buddies tackle reading issues, such as problem words.

Writing Journals

Standards
(See pages 122–23.)

- Writing

Guiding Concepts
(See pages viii–x.)

- Meaning making
- Intuitive knowing
- Emotion
- Creativity
- Self-reflection

Multiple Intelligences
(See page 124.)

- Verbal-linguistic
- Intrapersonal

Goals

- Students will practice spelling, grammar, and other mechanics of writing.
- Students will develop self-reflection and intrapersonal skills.
- Students will learn that one way to work out problems and difficult emotions is to find their own answers.

Time

15–30 minutes per day

Grade Range

K–8

Materials

✔ poster-size paper

✔ markers

✔ journals (make or buy)

✔ pens or pencils

✔ soft mood music (optional—see page 141 for suggestions)

Setup

Writing journals—communicating with myself.

Instructional Sequence

1. Explain to students that each will receive a special book. This book is special because it is a place to record thoughts, dreams, worries, cares, hopes, and anything else that is important. Tell students they will be able to look back on their books in years to come to see what they thought about and how they felt at this age. Someday they might have several journals that hold many of their special memories and thoughts from past years.

2. Pass out journals to all students and ask them to write their names on the fronts. Each student is responsible for his or her own journal for the year.

3. Brainstorm ideas for journal topics as a class and make a poster of these topics to which students can refer for ideas. For example, students could write about an event from the newspaper; any anger, sadness, or other emotions they need to work through; a problem with friends; discipline issues at school; and so forth.

4. Ask students to get a pencil or pen and find a quiet place to write for 10 minutes (to increase as the school year progresses, age appropriately). Play soft mood music during journal time (optional). Younger students could draw pictures, adding letters and words if they can.

5. Give students a chance to share a sentence or passage from their journals throughout the year (optional).

Assessment

This is a private, personal journal, so do not grade the spelling, grammar, and other mechanical details. Base your assessment on student effort to write for the entire period of time without talking or disrupting the class. Consider the following throughout the year:

- Are students able to write for longer periods of time as the year progresses?

- Do students think of ideas for writing topics on their own?

- Do students write about something they know?

- Do students use more detailed explanations and interesting vocabulary as the year progresses?

Variations

- Students could make the journals or decorate the covers using fabric scraps, sequins, recycled paper or cardboard, string, markers, and so forth.

- You could play different kinds of music and instruct students to write about emotions the music evokes.

- You could write a quotation on the board and ask students to write about what the quotation means to them.

- Students could use journal entries as poem or short story ideas in writer's workshop.

By all means, use sometimes to be alone.
Salute thyself: see what thy soul doth wear
Dare to look in thy chest, for 'tis thine own;
And tumble up and down what thou find'st there.

—George Herbert

Passionate Questions

Standards
(See pages 122–23.)

- Writing

Guiding Concepts
(See pages viii–x.)

- Meaning making
- Intuitive knowing
- Emotion
- Creativity
- Self-reflection

Multiple Intelligences
(See page 124.)

- Verbal-linguistic
- Intrapersonal

Goals

- Students will develop intrapersonal skills: They will learn about themselves and how to listen to their inner voices.

- Students will communicate effectively using writing; with descriptive language, they will paint a vivid picture.

- Students will learn about poetry and think of themselves as poets.

- You will have the opportunity to learn about students' passions and can choose activities, topics, books, and so forth with these passions in mind.

Time

2 hours

Grade Range

3–8

Materials

- ✔ paper and pencil for each student
- ✔ large piece of white construction paper (or a computer with printer)
- ✔ pens, crayons, or pastels
- ✔ the book *I Wonder* by Hoban (or another book of questions, such as *How Come?*, by Wollard, or *The Kids' Book of Questions*, by Stock)

I wonder what birds dream about.

Setup

Read *I Wonder* (or another book of questions) and think about questions you have that have no easy answers. What are you really passionate about learning? Your questions could be concrete, such as "Why do stars twinkle?," or abstract, such as "Why can't we all live in peace?" or "Why aren't people nice to each other?"

Instructional Sequence

1. Begin a discussion about questions that have no easy answers. You may want to share some of your own questions or start by reading from a book about questions, such as *I Wonder*. If you read from a book that gives answers as well as questions, read just the questions. You could read the answers later as part of a follow-up activity if you wish.

2. Explain that each student will write a poem about his or her unanswered questions. Each line will begin with a question word: why, how, where, who, or when. For example: Why is the sky blue? Students can use the same question word (with different questions) throughout the poem or they can vary the question words. Assign a required length as appropriate for the age group (such as a minimum of five questions).

3. Stress that the questions should focus on something students feel passionate about, something they really wonder about. Ask students: "If you could have the answer to any question, what would the question be?"

4. After editing their poems, students make nice copies (with pens and white construction paper or on computer) to display or to take home.

Assessment

Assess the process as well as the poem itself:

- Do students participate in class discussion?

- Do students use descriptive, colorful words in their poems?

- Do students really think about what they passionately want to know?

- Do students apply the writing traits (ideas, organization, voice, word choice, sentence fluency, conventions, presentation) as appropriate?

- Do students edit their poems for mechanical errors, such as spelling, grammar, and punctuation?

- Do students put care into their final products?

Variations

- Students could try a short story that provides fictional answers to their questions or an essay that delves into the true answers to their questions.

- You could focus this activity on a particular category, such as questions about animals, plants, the human body, the Earth, the universe, and so forth.

- You could make this an ongoing journal assignment, with students writing entries about one question per week.

- Students could create a painting or collage that represents the question about which they are most interested. Pieces could also include possible answers and the real answer (if there is one).

- Younger students (K–2) could write a class poem, with you guiding the process and writing the poem (on the board or on poster paper).

> *Live your questions now and perhaps, even without knowing it, you will live along some distant day into your answers.*
> —R. M. Rilke

More Reading and Writing Activity Ideas_____

- Students could keep "field" journals throughout a unit to record thoughts, feelings, fears, questions, and so forth.

- Students could study and write personal credos.

- The class could look for connections between poetry and art, perhaps with a focus on religious poetry and art from cultures around the world.

- Students could seek found poems and describe why their poems are meaningful to them. (*Found poems* are poems made from words and phrases that are already written. You literally find them in prose passages or more unusual locations, such as in graffiti or on signs.)

- Students could write "A day in the life of . . ." about spiritual or cultural leaders.

- The class could hold a storytelling round: The class chooses a favorite story and each student memorizes a portion of the story. They then take turns telling the story to another class (or the school).

- You could combine reading, writing, and problem-solving by having students write each week in their journals about a problem or issue in school or their personal lives. Assign personal reading to help each student address his or her particular issue. For example, if a student is having problems with a bully, you might assign Bottner and Rathman's *Bootsie Barker Bites* or Hahn's *Stepping on the Cracks*.

- Students could write book reports on books that deal with character or other spiritual issues, such as those listed on pages 136–41. Reports could focus on how the books parallel (or don't parallel) students' lives and how the books affect them personally.

- You could read parts of the book *Important Things,* by Springer, and have each student write about (and illustrate with photographs) an important thing in his or her life. Create a class book with writing pieces and photos.

Add your own ideas:

Chapter 2

Science and Math Activities

Drinking Flower

Standards
(See pages 122–23.)

- Writing
- Science

Guiding Concepts
(See pages viii–x.)

- Intuitive knowing
- Connections
- Nature

Multiple Intelligences
(See page 124.)

- Verbal-linguistic
- Logical-mathematical
- Naturalist

Goals

- Students will make the connection that what we do to the Earth, we do to ourselves because we are all interconnected.
- Students will learn how plants use water.

Time

1 hour work time and 1 hour wait time

Grade Range

1–4

Materials

- ✔ pale carnations (one for each group of three to five students)
- ✔ food coloring for each group
- ✔ glass of water for each group
- ✔ observation journal for each student (make or buy)

Setup

Put a carnation, a glass of water, and some food coloring on each table. (If your classroom doesn't have tables, push together four desks.)

Instructional Sequence

1. Instruct students to form small groups, then get out their journals and write down what they notice about the flower at their group's table. Ask them to consider their senses (smell, sight, touch). For students just learning to write, discuss observations as a class and write student observations on the board.

2. When class discussion is complete, or when all students at a table are finished with their descriptions, each group should put food coloring in the water and put the stem of the flower in the water. (Before lunch is a good time for this.)

3. After an hour has passed, ask the students to again record or discuss what they notice about the flower, which will have turned colors as it soaked up the colored water. Ask them to write down or tell you what they think has happened.

4. After students are finished, bring them back into one group to discuss their findings. Ask questions as necessary to help them along: "Do you notice anything about the color of the water and the color of your flower?" "Why do you think the flower turned colors?"

"What do plants need to survive?" Guide them as necessary to the conclusion that flowers "drink" water to live, and therefore they also drink whatever is in the water (such as food coloring). To help explain and solidify the concepts, you could read a book to the class about how plants grow, such as *The Magic School Bus Plants Seeds: A Book About How Living Things Grow*, by Cole, or *Plants Feed on Sunlight: And Other Facts about Things That Grow*, by Taylor.

5. Ask students if they think other plants might change color if you added food coloring to their water. Ask students what would happen to the plant if there were pesticides or other chemicals in the water.

6. Discuss the impact of humans on the environment and how we hurt ourselves when we hurt the environment. (For example, we eat the plants that drink the water, therefore contaminating ourselves if we contaminate the water.)

7. Ask students if they have ideas about what we could do to make the environment cleaner. They could write these ideas in their journals or create a picture or sentence to display.

Assessment

During and after this activity, consider these questions:

- Do students follow directions and work well in a group?

- Do students use critical thinking (in their journals and in discussion) to try to figure out what has happened to the flower?

- Do students express themselves clearly verbally and orally?

- Do students understand human impact on the environment as demonstrated in this activity?

Variations

- The class could create posters or write poems or songs that address human impact on the environment, particularly in relation to water.

- You could try this activity as part of a larger plant unit, in which students try other experiments to see the effects of heat, light (or lack of light), and different air quality on a plant. For example, students could grow two plants, one in the daylight and one in a dark corner, one in a cooler filled with ice and one under a heat lamp, or one treated with herbicide and one untreated.

- You could discuss the sources of water pollution (such as household chemicals, industrial waste, and pesticides) and potential solutions: using biodegradable household cleansers, for example, or writing to local and state representatives about pollution-related laws.

- Students could learn how to dry flowers using the carnations (and perhaps additional flowers you bring in).

- Older students could try this activity as an introduction to a unit on human impact on the Earth. This unit would include research and writing about ways humans affect the earth, such as use of local waterways, practices that cause acid rain, and so forth.

- You could take the class on a field trip to an organic farm, with a question-and-answer session at the farm or after the trip about the benefits of organic farming.

Life Circle

Standards
(See pages 122–23.)
- Science
- Social studies

Guiding Concepts
(See pages viii–x.)
- Meaning making
- Connections
- Nature

Multiple Intelligences
(See page 124.)
- Visual-spatial
- Interpersonal
- Naturalist

Goals

- Students will begin to understand the effects of humans on other creatures.
- Students will observe nature, draw conclusions, and learn to make decisions that will make the world a better place.

Time

6 hours over 1 week

Grade Range

K–4

Materials

- ✔ several pieces of yarn or wire (each long enough to make a circle with a yard circumference)
- ✔ observation journals (make or buy)
- ✔ reference books about local insects, plants, and animals, with pictures (check with the school librarian for books related to your area; see also the suggestions on page 138)
- ✔ crayons or pastels (if students draw in journals)
- ✔ paper and pens (if students write poems, essays, songs, or short stories)
- ✔ glue and construction paper (if students create a photo montage)

Setup

Set up a yarn or wire circle on the playground early in the day. Anchor yarn with rocks. Inform other teachers about the lesson so they can ask their students not to disturb the circle. Put up a sign to remind people that the circle is an important part of an ongoing experiment.

Instructional Sequence

1. Hand out observation journals and explain that the class will be taking some trips outside to observe nature.

2. In the afternoon, have students go out in small groups with an adult supervisor (or go out as a class) and record what they see inside the circle (insects, leaves that have fallen, and so forth). Students just learning to write can also draw pictures. On some playgrounds, students may see nothing in the circle. "Nothing" is an important observation. It will be valuable to compare this

observation with those performed in a park or backyard.

3. On another day, take a field trip to a park and set up a yarn circle there. After about 30 minutes, have students again record what they see inside the circle (with words or pictures). During the 30-minute waiting period, the class could have a picnic, a nature walk, or a class discussion about what students observe at the park (including sight, sound, touch, and smell, as well as emotions evoked).

4. For homework, give each student two pieces of yarn to set up observation circles at home—one on a driveway or sidewalk and one in a natural area, such as woods or desert. Students should record what they see once a day for three days.

5. Have a class discussion about what they saw. Did they see more in the park or on the playground? At home, did they see more on pavement or in natural areas?

6. Ask students why they think there is more life in the park or other natural areas.

7. Lead a discussion about habitat, what other living things need to survive, and what effect humans have on their existence. For example, if students saw nothing in the circle on the playground, you could discuss why (trees can't grow in cement, insects and other animals need food and shelter, and so forth), then discuss why they saw more at the park (because a natural habitat exists). Choose a

particular insect or tree students observed and focus on the details of its habitat and what it needs to thrive.

8. Talk about what kinds of things students can do to have a positive influence on the environment and other living things. For example, you could discuss recycling; not littering; planting to replenish habitats; planting new habitats; being careful about what goes down the drain (such as chemicals); being kind to living things (not tearing leaves off trees or killing insects for fun); conserving energy, paper, water, and food; and teaching others what they have learned.

9. Have students write poems, songs, essays, or short stories about what they have learned and what they think they can do to have a positive influence. Younger students could create a photo montage or draw pictures to illustrate what they have learned. Make a book of all the students' work.

Students and teachers created this habitat in a corner of a cement playground to attract local wildlife.

Assessment

Consider the following questions during the field trips and in your evaluation of student work:

- Do students follow directions as demonstrated by the notes or drawings in their journals and their final pieces?

- Do students treat each other with respect on the field trips?

- Do students participate in class discussions (listening and contributing their own ideas)?

- In final written pieces, do students use the writing process (prewriting, drafting, revising, editing, publishing)?

- In final written pieces, how well do students use the writing traits (ideas, organization, voice, word choice, sentence fluency, conventions, presentation)?

- Do nonwritten final pieces relate to the topic and demonstrate an understanding of habitats?

- Do students demonstrate an understanding of the connection and impact that humans have with and on the Earth and other living things?

Variations

- You could tie this activity into a larger unit on the study of habitats. Students could research local insects and birds and create a habitat in a corner of the playground to attract wildlife. Creating a habitat might involve planting trees and other plants, building a bird house and fountain, and so forth.

- In small groups, students could focus on a particular category of living creatures for further study and presentation. For example, one group might focus on plants, another on insects, another on birds, another on sea creatures, and so forth.

- Students could compare elements of their own habitats to those of another living creature. For example, students might compare their homes and basic survival needs to those of a particular bird found in your region. They might consider what would endanger their own habitats.

- You could expand this activity into a discussion of the different types of world habitats, such as temperate forest, tropical rain forest, desert, arctic regions, and savannas.

- Students could observe the life circles throughout the entire year, keeping detailed journals that include observing life cycles (such as those of insects or birds) and the effects of seasonal changes.

- Students might create a larger life circle to encompass a greater area.

> *Miracles are not contrary to nature, but only contrary to what we know about nature.*
>
> —St. Augustine of Hippo

Knowing Myself

Standards
(See pages 122–23.)

- Writing
- Science
- Health and fitness

Guiding Concepts
(See pages viii–x.)

- Intuitive knowing
- Emotion
- Connections
- Self-reflection

Multiple Intelligences
(See page 124.)

- Verbal-linguistic
- Logical-mathematical
- Bodily-kinesthetic
- Intrapersonal

Goals

- Students will learn how to be aware of their bodies.
- Students will learn how food, sleep, emotions, exercise, and other life factors affect them.

Time

1–2 hours spread over 3 weeks

Grade Range

2–8

Materials

- ✔ journals (make or buy)
- ✔ reference books about the body, nutrition, and exercise (see suggestions on page 138)
- ✔ poster paper and markers or pastels (optional)

Setup

Put reference books in a visible place, accessible to all students.

Instructional Sequence

1. Pass out journals and ask students to write a few sentences or jot down a few phrases about their bodies (preassessment of how well they know themselves). They should write down whatever comes to mind: how they feel about their bodies, how healthy they feel, what makes them feel bad or good,

I feel strong when I play outside.

and so forth. If necessary, stress that students should take the assignment seriously in order to learn more about themselves (and to do well on the project).

2. Ask if anyone wants to share an idea from the journal.

3. Ask students what kinds of things might affect their bodies and how they feel, such as exercise, food, sleep, emotions, hygiene, relaxation time, and so forth. Brainstorm as a class and write ideas on the board.

4. Give or ask for an example of an emotion that affects the body. (For example, feeling sad or happy can cause a person to cry.)

5. Tell students that for the next three weeks, they will keep detailed journals about themselves. The journals will include information about food (what they eat every day), exercise, emotions, and all the other things you've brainstormed.

6. Explain that during the first week, they will observe their normal routines and habits. They should write in their journals at least three times a day.

7. After each entry, they will write down how each action has made them feel. (For example: "I ate a huge piece of cake. I feel kind of sick to my stomach. My face feels greasy, like all that fat is coming through my pores. I feel bad because I didn't have the willpower to stop at half a piece.")

8. Point out the reference books and let students know to look up things in which they are interested, such as different types of exercise or the effects of different foods on the body.

9. During the second and third weeks, students can try to make changes to their routines and habits to get positive results. For example: Add an afternoon walk or 15 minutes of quiet time a day; try to think positive thoughts; floss every day; read instead of watch TV; and so on.

10. Periodically check in with students both as a class and individually to see how things are going, what they've noticed, whether they have questions or need help thinking of changes to make, whether they are on task, and so forth.

11. At the end of the three weeks, have students read through their journals and draw some conclusions about their findings. For example, they might examine which changes they made worked or did not work to solve particular problems or to enhance how they felt. They should present their findings in some fashion, such as a report, a poster, poems, a play, or a story.

Assessment

Consider the following questions throughout the three-week exercise:

- Do students write in their journals often (three times a day minimum)?

- Do students take the project seriously and show an interest in learning about themselves?

- Are students able to recognize what affects their bodies and how they feel?

- Are students able to draw connections between what they observe or feel about their bodies and what actions they can take to change their observations or feelings?

- Consider the following questions when you evaluate student presentations:

- Do students clearly present their findings and draw some conclusions?

- If the final presentation is written, do students use the writing process (prewriting, drafting, revising, editing, publishing) and develop the writing traits (ideas, organization, voice, word choice, sentence fluency, conventions, presentation)?

> *If any thing is sacred, the human body is sacred.*
> —Walt Whitman

Variations

- Students could keep their journals for a longer period.

- Students could write about assigned daily topics in addition to daily observations. For example, you might assign a different body part for students to research and write about each day, starting with their heads and ending with their toes.

- The class could take a field trip to different healthcare facilities (traditional, such as a hospital, and alternative, such as an acupuncture clinic) or invite guest speakers with expertise in some area of health.

- For extra credit, students could cut white sugar and white flour from their diet for a week and write about their experiences. (They will have to understand and read food labels for this project.)

Fresh air and exercise help me stay healthy.

Flower Sets _____

Standards
(See pages 122–23.)

- Math
- Science

Guiding Concepts
(See pages viii–x.)

- Emotion
- Connections
- Nature

Multiple Intelligences
(See page 124.)

- Logical-mathematical
- Visual-spatial
- Naturalist

Goals

Students will learn about the mathematical concept of sets while enjoying the beauty of flowers and music.

Time

1 hour

Grade Range

K–2

Materials

- ✔ one basket of different kinds of flowers—different sizes, shapes, colors, and so forth—for each group of five students (if on a budget, collect wildflowers, ask kids to bring flowers from home, or seek donations from local hotels or restaurants)
- ✔ smaller baskets, vases, or other containers
- ✔ soft mood music (see page 141 for possible selections)
- ✔ index cards
- ✔ pencils or pens

Setup

- ▪ Put a basket of flowers in a variety of colors and shapes on each of four tables (or on each of four groups of desks).
- ▪ Put several small containers on each table as well (one for each student).

Instructional Sequence

1. As a class, review the concept of sets. Use your school's math books or see the suggested title on page 137. You could also demonstrate the concept of sets by sorting various items into sets as a class, such as colored blocks, blocks of different shapes, children dressed in long sleeves and children dressed in short sleeves, and so forth.

2. Explain that students will get to make their own flower arrangements, but they will be arranging flowers into sets (organized by shape or color, for example). Each student gets to choose what kind of set his or her arrangement represents.

3. Play soft mood music while students work with the flowers.

4. When they are finished with their arrangements, students will use index cards to make signs that explain their sets. (For example, a blue set, a circle set, or a five-petal set.)

5. When everyone is finished, students walk around and look at their classmates' arrangements and explanations.

6. Have a discussion about the process. Assess understanding of sets; discuss other ways sets could be used; and discuss what it was like to work with the flowers and music (such as effects on mood and emotion).

Assessment

Consider the following questions during and after the activity:

- Do students work cooperatively with the group at their table (such as sharing flowers fairly)?

- Do students seem to enjoy the music and flowers?

- Do students understand sets as demonstrated by their flower arrangements and explanations?

Variations

- Instead of flowers, students could group together other natural objects, such as dry beans, leaves, seashells, or seeds. Students could also group pictures of natural objects, such as flowers, animals, sunsets, babies, and seashells.

- Students could look at other students' sets and try to guess the unifying characteristics, instead of writing explanations for the arrangements.

- The class could take a field trip to bring their flower arrangements to people in a hospice, hospital, or senior citizen home.

- Expand the discussion of sets to talk about how and why people group themselves and each other into sets (such as cliques and clubs) based on their similarities.

Flowers and music make learning fun.

Giving a Million

Standards
(See pages 122–23.)
- Communication
- Math
- Art

Guiding Concepts
(See pages viii–x.)
- Meaning making
- Character
- Connections

Multiple Intelligences
(See page 124.)
- Logical-mathematical
- Interpersonal

Goals

- Students will expand their concept of large numbers.
- Students will work together for a worthy cause, exploring ideas about charity, helping others, and working together toward a common goal.

Time

2 hours a week for 4 weeks

Grade Range

K–3

Materials

- ✔ *How Much is a Million?*, by Schwartz (or *If You Made a Million,* by Schwartz)
- ✔ *The Rajah's Rice,* by Barry (optional)
- ✔ a large bucket
- ✔ 3' x 5' sheet of butcher paper (for class adding poster)
- ✔ large sheet of construction paper (for class card)
- ✔ bag of beads (or dry beans)
- ✔ pens, crayons, or pastels
- ✔ paper (for poems or pictures about the experience)
- ✔ sandwich bags or other container for beads

Setup

- Choose a charity (such as a senior citizen home, the charity in this example). Contact the charity to arrange regular class visits and to discuss specific rules and ways students can help.
- Send letters to parents and guardians explaining that the class is learning about helping others. The class will visit the senior citizen home periodically (once a week if possible).
- Write "We can help others by donating our time" at the top of the sheet of paper and hang it up in the classroom, low enough for students to reach but high enough for the entire class to see. Be sure to leave room on the paper for more writing. This will be the class adding poster.
- At the beginning of class, set out the bucket at the front of the room. Put 10 beads (or beans) in one pocket and 5 in another.

Instructional Sequence

1. Begin a discussion about large numbers to get a baseline level of understanding in the class. Read *How Much Is a Million* to the class.

2. Point out the big bucket and the sign you hung up and tell students they will try to donate a million minutes to help others, and they will keep track by collecting beads. Each bead will represent one minute.

3. Ask them how full they think the bucket will be at the end of the project.

4. Explain that they will visit the senior citizen home periodically. Discuss with the class what this visit entails, such as talking with people (asking questions and listening), playing games, helping people move around the home (if students are able), and any other ideas the home may have given you. Each student will add the same number of beads to the bucket as the minutes he or she spent helping others.

5. Take 10 beads from your pocket and count them in front of the class. Drop the beads into the bucket and write "10" on the adding poster. Take out 5 beads from the other pocket, count them for the students, write "+ 5 =," and ask for answers from students. Then write "15" on the poster. Explain that 15 beads represents 15 minutes. (For younger children, adding new beads could be a whole class exercise; older students could add beads and keep track of numbers on the poster independently.)

6. Explain the process and make sure students understand. To check understanding, ask volunteers to explain the process. You could also try a class activity with students counting beads at their desks and recording the equations on paper.

7. Visit the home each week and, periodically, put the beads into bags of 25 or 100 (choose students to count out the correct number of beads) to show how large amounts can be grouped for easier handling. You could read *The Rajah's Rice* at this time to solidify the concept of grouping.

8. Have students draw pictures or write poems that represent the process. The pictures or poems could be either math-related or charity-related (or both). Post them on a bulletin board or wall.

9. At the end of the month (or whatever length of time you choose), count how many beads you have actually collected and have a class discussion about how it feels to donate time to others. What did students give? What did they receive? How can they continue giving when the school project is done? Do they think they could reach one million beads if they kept donating time until the end of the school year?

10. Have students make and sign a big class card that thanks the senior citizen home for inviting them to visit.

I helped someone today!

Assessment

Evaluate understanding of the math involved in this activity:

- During class discussions, do students demonstrate understanding of counting and of beads representing minutes?

- Do students contribute to counting and adding the number of beads?

- Do students show understanding of books read during this activity?

- Do students apply their understanding when estimating how long it will take for them to collect a million beads?

Evaluate understanding of and participation in community service:

- Do students demonstrate an understanding of charity and community service, such as why they should help others and the intangible rewards involved in helping others?

- Do students participate and respect others at the senior citizen home?

- Do students consider ways they can continue to help others outside of class?

Variations

- Instead of donating time, the class could collect pennies (count as described above) and donate the money to a charity.

- Students could continue to donate time outside of school and add beads to the bucket. You could brainstorm as a class the many organizations and people who could use student help.

- Students could create a large colorful graph to show their progress in collecting beads throughout the year.

- The class could discuss large numbers in other contexts, such as how many drops of water from an eyedropper it would take to fill a bucket, or how many grains of sand will fit in a cup. Students could then imagine how many drops of water are in an ocean and how many grains of sand are on a beach.

- Students could learn about fractions, ratios, division, multiplication, and other mathematical operations using this activity as a starting point. For example, students could figure out the average number of beads each student has contributed overall, each week and each month. Then they could figure out how long it would take to get to a million if only $1/3$ of the class participated (then $1/4$ $1/8$, and so forth).

> *Did universal charity prevail, earth would be a heaven, and hell a fable.*
>
> —Charles Caleb Colton

Math in Nature

Standards
(See pages 122–23.)
- Writing
- Math
- Science

Guiding Concepts
(See pages viii–x.)
- Creativity
- Connections
- Self-reflection
- Nature

Multiple Intelligences
(See page 124.)
- Verbal-linguistic
- Logical-mathematical
- Visual-spatial
- Naturalist

Goals

- Students will find patterns in nature and enjoy being outdoors.
- Students will express their ideas and observations through poetry.

Time

2 hours' class time, plus a half-day field trip

Grade Range

1–4

Materials

- ✔ journals (make or buy)
- ✔ different items from nature, such as leaves, rocks, shells, flowers, pictures of animals (such as butterflies)
- ✔ 3 or 4 disposable cameras labeled with letters
- ✔ *The Important Book,* by M. W. Brown
- ✔ Computer and printer or paper and colorful markers

Setup

- Organize a field trip to a park or other place with trees, flowers, shells, or other natural items that will demonstrate mathematical ideas such as symmetry, sets, geometry, and patterns.
- Select a few objects to use as examples for the class. You could use a leaf to demonstrate symmetry, a cactus to demonstrate asymmetry, a picture of a spotted or striped animal to demonstrate patterns, a round rock to demonstrate geometric shapes, and a collection of similar flowers to demonstrate sets.

Instructional Sequence

1. Gather students in a circle on the floor and put several items on the floor (leaves, shells, rocks, flowers, pictures of butterflies, and so on) and ask students what they notice about the items. Are any similar? Are there patterns?

2. Show students the items you selected and explain how they demonstrate symmetry, patterns, and so forth.

3. Explain that the class will be going on a field trip to gather pictures of natural things that demonstrate symmetry, patterns, geometric shapes, and so forth.

4. Read *The Important Book* and discuss how the book describes something using many details and then chooses one detail on which to focus.

5. Tell students they will take journals with them on the field trip. As they find things that demonstrate the mathematical concepts, they will write down some attributes of what they find so they can create a poem later. They should include things such as how the item makes them feel, what it reminds them of, how it smells, and so forth. You might give examples using the items you selected. For example, "This cactus reminds me of a porcupine. Its smell makes me think of visiting New Mexico with my family."

6. After they finish taking notes about an item, they should ask you for one of the cameras. They take a picture of the item and then write down next to their notes the camera letter and the picture number. That way you can match the picture to the poem when the pictures are developed.

7. After the field trip, students will write their poems in the same format Brown uses in *The Important Book*, edit them for spelling and other errors, and make a final copy on the computer or on paper, using markers.

8. Students can share their work with each other and then post the poems with the corresponding photos for the school to enjoy. You could also collect the poems and photos in a class book.

Assessment

During and after the field trip, keep the following questions in mind:

- Do students use the writing process (prewriting, drafting, revising, editing, publishing) and develop the writing traits (ideas, organization, voice, word choice, sentence fluency, conventions, presentation) in their poems?

- Do students take detailed notes and show an understanding of mathematical ideas by choosing objects that accurately represent mathematical concepts?

- Do students treat nature with respect?

- Do students express their ideas well in writing and does their writing demonstrate an ability to describe things they see, hear, smell, and feel?

Young gardeners look for patterns in nature.

Variations

- Instead of taking photographs of elements in nature, students could do rubbings or draw them in their journals.

- Students could write poems in forms that reflect a pattern they found in nature. For example, students might write two symmetrical columns of a poem that form the shape of a leaf, or a series of short poems that each have something in common to create a set.

- You could prepare cards for this activity that demonstrate visually the different patterns you want students to look for in nature. Include an example of each shape, an example of symmetry, an example of asymmetry, and so forth. Show the students the cards to discuss (or review) the mathematical concepts before showing examples from nature.

- You could expand the activity to include looking for mathematical concepts in the human body. Students could examine themselves for patterns, sets, shapes, symmetry, asymmetry, and so forth.

A student discovers math through nature and expresses her new understanding in a poem.

> *Come forth into the light of things.*
> *Let nature be your teacher.*
> —William Wordsworth

More Science and Math Activity Ideas _____

- Your class could take regular nature walks or one long nature walk.

- You could invite guest speakers to discuss the illnesses of students in your class.

- Students could care for a class pet.

- Students could keep math journals: Students figure out problems in math journals and then share their journals with partners or small groups, helping each other and sharing strategies with the class.

- The class could cook for the homeless: Students learn about fractions by following recipes to make food (such as stew) or entire meals for the homeless.

- Students could create inventions (similar to Rube Goldberg machines) out of miscellaneous materials (such as craft sticks, rubber bands, pieces of cloth, toy cars, balloons, paperclips, and so forth) to learn about chain reactions and reinforce lessons about interconnectedness. Assign a type of invention (such as a machine to pour water or transport an object from one place in the room to another), or have students design whatever machine they can come up with using the materials on hand.

- Students could play math games (such as dominos, cards, any game with dice, Monopoly, and so forth) to work on both math and cooperative learning skills.

- You could take a class field trip to the zoo or an aquarium to observe animals. Ask students to consider how the animals' lives might be different in their natural habitats.

Add your own ideas:

Chapter 3
Art and Music Activities

I Would Be Good

Standards

(See pages 122–23.)

- Writing
- Art

Guiding Concepts

(See pages viii–x.)

- Intuitive knowing
- Character
- Emotion
- Creativity
- Connections
- Self-reflection

Multiple Intelligences

(See page 124.)

- Verbal-linguistic
- Musical-rhythmic
- Intrapersonal

Goals

- Students will think about things they fear and begin to realize they can handle much more than they think they can, and they can trust their own feelings and ideas.
- Students will work on their verbal comprehension skills.

Time

1–2 hours

Grade Range

4–8

Materials

- ✔ recording of "That I Would Be Good" by Alanis Morissette
- ✔ paper
- ✔ pens or pencils

Setup

If it's not possible to use a recording of Morissette's song, bring in a copy of the lyrics to read to the class.

Instructional Sequence

1. Play (or read) the song for the class.

2. Ask students what they noticed about the song. (For example: Most lines start with "That I would be good" and she talks about things she wouldn't like to have happen.) You may need to hang up a poster of the lyrics and replay the song.

3. Talk about what students think the lesson of the song is (basically, I will be fine even if the worst thing I can imagine happens to me). Discuss how they can use this idea in their own lives.

4. Tell students they will write songs or poems about their fears.

5. They can begin by brainstorming some ideas. You could provide a few examples (such as fear of heights, fear of meeting new people, and so forth) and ask students for a few examples.

6. After they have some ideas about their own fears down on paper, they can begin to organize them into poems or songs. They can model their poems or songs after Morissette's style or choose a style of their own.

7. After editing for spelling and other possible errors, students should make a final copy. They can decorate it if they choose.

Assessment

Throughout this activity, keep the following questions in mind:

- Do students listen to the words of the song and comprehend what the message is (older students may be able to draw more conclusions than younger students)?

- Do students put thought and care into their own pieces?

- Do students use the writing process (prewriting, drafting, revising, editing, publishing) and pay attention to the writing traits (ideas, organization, voice, word choice, sentence fluency, conventions, presentation)?

- Are students able to think critically about their own fears and concerns?

Variations

- You could use a different song with a similar or different message or style.

- Students could include ways of conquering their fears in their poems or songs.

- Students could create a class poem: Sit in a circle and start off the class with the beginning of a line (such as "I would be good if . . ." or "I'd be happy even if . . ."). Each student takes a turn completing the line as you go around the circle.

- Instead of a poem or song, students could create a painting, drawing, or comic strip that depicts their fear and shows them conquering it.

> *No passion so effectually robs the mind of all its powers of acting and reasoning as fear.*
> —Edmund Burke

Rotating Art

Standards
(See pages 122–23.)

- Communication
- Art

Guiding Concepts
(See pages viii–x.)

- Character
- Emotion
- Creativity
- Connections

Multiple Intelligences
(See page 124.)

- Visual-spatial
- Interpersonal

Goals

Students will build community and respect for others by working on a class art project in groups.

Time

1 hour

Grade Range

K–8

Materials

- ✔ five large pieces of paper
- ✔ markers, crayons, pencils, or pastels
- ✔ five different sets of the same stickers (enough total stickers for all students in the class)
- ✔ paper and pencils or pens (for reflection pieces)
- ✔ index cards

Setup

- Put the five pieces of paper on five tables around the room.
- Put supplies on each table.
- Put the stickers on index cards (one card per student) to group students.

Instructional Sequence

1. Pass out cards to students and ask them to get into groups based on the stickers on their cards. As a group they should choose a table at which to work.

2. Explain that they will be making five different pictures of the same object. Choose something special to your class, such as a mascot or class animal.

3. They will start by drawing an outline of the object, then add details. Every student in the group should contribute to the picture.

4. After five minutes, the groups will move clockwise to the next table and continue with the picture that was started by the last group. This rotation continues until all groups have contributed to each picture.

5. When the process is complete, gather the group in a circle for a discussion of the process. For a new class, this process will show how well the students know how to work in groups and how much each student respects his or her own and others' work. A teacher can gain much information from observing this activity.

Some emotions may come out during the discussion if some students didn't respect the work that was previously done. Guide the discussion as you feel is appropriate. Students will benefit from learning how to address emotions and issues respectfully as a class.

6. Hang the pictures on the classroom wall. Tell the students, "This is what you have created as a class."

7. Ask students to write a reflection piece (one or two paragraphs) discussing what they have learned about themselves, their class, cooperation, pride, and so forth.

8. Do the same process two more times during the year to see class community growth.

Assessment

During and after the activity, consider the following questions:

- Do students follow directions?

- Do students work well in a group and respect each other's work?

- How do students react to emotional situations (if the process results in high emotions)?

- Do students demonstrate any knowledge of art concepts (such as use of space, shading, perspective, texture, and color)? Note: Younger students' drawings will probably be simple, two-dimensional, and colorful. Older students will begin to use perspective, shading, and texture.

Variations

- Students could try a rotating story project, with groups each starting a story at a table and then moving around from table to table, continuing each group's story.

- In a small class, students could work on art as individuals, instead of in groups.

- You could make this an ongoing art project. Keep a large sheet of paper on a table or hung on the wall throughout the quarter, semester, or year. Start the artwork as a class. Students can then add to it individually as the year progresses.

- Start the art project with a few random lines, loops, and shapes on the paper. Students then create what they see out of what's already on the paper, rather than drawing a set object.

We don't live alone. We are members of one body. We are responsible for each other.
—J. B. Priestley

Me Puzzle

Standards
(See pages 122–23.)
- Communication
- Art

Guiding Concepts
(See pages viii–x.)
- Creativity
- Self-reflection

Multiple Intelligences
(See page 124.)
- Visual-spatial
- Intrapersonal

Goals

- Students will learn that human development includes six components: physical, cognitive, emotional, social, aesthetic, and spiritual.
- Students will reflect on each of these areas within themselves and construct a me puzzle.

Time

3 hours' work time, plus presentation time

Grade Range

5–8

Materials

- ✔ cardboard boxes (enough for each student to make a 3′ x 3′ cut-out person for his or her puzzle—each puzzle will have 6 pieces)
- ✔ many different kinds of fabric or wallpaper with pictures, designs, themes, and so forth (Students could bring some from home.)
- ✔ glue sticks and staplers
- ✔ journals or reflection pages
- ✔ pens or pencils

Setup

- Make a me puzzle of your own (3′ x 3′ or larger) and bring it to class. If you teach younger students, create a puzzle template for them to use when cutting out their pieces.

I'm special!

- You could create reflection pages for students by writing each human development component on separate sheets of paper with space for students to write.

- You could read up on human development theories. See *Educational Psychology*, by Anita Woolfolk (2000), for example, in the reference list on page 143.

Instructional Sequence

1. Put your puzzle in the front of the room. Ask students if they can guess what it is.

   After listening to their ideas about what it is, explain that it is a me puzzle and that it represents the six components of human development.

2. Ask students if they can name some of the ways in which humans develop. Write the ideas on the board and add any they don't come up with.

3. Explain the six components of human development. The box on this page contains some basic definitions you could use as a starting point.

4. Go over your puzzle and explain each piece and why you chose to decorate it the way you did. For example, the piece representing physical development might have a covering with sneakers on it if you run. Your spiritual development piece might have a white cloth to represent silence and light.

5. Explain that the students will make their own puzzles based on their personal ideas about the six developmental components. They will spend some time thinking and writing about how best to represent themselves. (Pass out reflection pages or use journals.)

6. Put out cardboard, fabric, glue sticks, and staplers and give students time to work on their projects. Set out a puzzle template for younger students.

7. Have students present their puzzles to the class, explaining each piece.

Assessment

Throughout this activity, consider the following questions:

- Do students use self-reflection time productively?

- Can students explain why they decorated their puzzles the way they did?

- Do students present their ideas clearly?

- Do students put care and effort into creating their puzzles?

Six Components of Human Development

Physical: the health and development of a person's body, including muscle strength, coordination, gross and fine motor skills, and so forth

Cognitive: the development of how people remember what they see and hear, think about problems they encounter, predict what might happen in the future, comprehend what they read, understand the similarities and differences between different ideas and objects, and create solutions for problems that puzzle them

Emotional: the development of the means by which a person learns to appraise the significance of stimuli to prepare the body for an appropriate response, including the ability to devote energy to self-understanding, to be aware of or responsive to others, and to understand the effect of personal actions

Social: the development of an individual's ability to respond to other people, situations, and themselves in ways that show respect, care, concern, and commitment to what is fair and just in society

Aesthetic: the development of the ability to appreciate beauty; use art as an expression of feelings; enjoy music, dance, poetry, and so forth; and use creativity and imagination to solve problems

Spiritual: the development of the need and desire to fulfill oneself, to become all one is capable of becoming, and to find the meaning and purpose of life

Variations

- Instead of using cardboard pieces, you could draw the outlines of students on large rolls of white paper. Students then cut out and fill in their outlines with drawings and pictures to illustrate the six components of development.

- You could cut out student puzzle pieces in advance and have students work on each component of development as a separate project, without telling them that the pieces will all come together in the end. This would enable you to spend more time focusing on each component.

- Students could write an essay about each component in their puzzles.

- Students could create puzzles in shapes of their own choosing, abstract or concrete shapes that they think reflect who they are.

- Instead of using fabric for the entire puzzle, students could vary tools and media for each piece, such as painting to express spiritual development, a collage to express cognitive development, construction paper to express physical development, and so on. Students could also use magazine pictures and photos of themselves instead of fabric.

- The class could create one giant puzzle that reflects each member. Before class begins, cut puzzle pieces (so that each student gets one) out of a large sheet of cardboard or a large sheet of paper. Students decorate their own pieces in a way that illustrates who they think they are (self-portrait, or things they like, or something more abstract). Then you put the pieces together into one large work of art.

Self-Portrait

Standards
(See pages 122–23.)
- Art

Guiding Concepts
(See pages viii–x.)
- Creativity
- Self-reflection

Multiple Intelligences
(See page 124.)
- Visual-spatial
- Intrapersonal
- Interpersonal

Goals
- Students will use art and both interpersonal and intrapersonal skills to introduce themselves to others.
- Self-portraits can also show how students feel about themselves.

Time
1–2 hours

Grade Range
K–8

Materials
- ✔ white construction paper (11 x 17)
- ✔ pencils
- ✔ erasers
- ✔ pastels or colored pencils
- ✔ mirrors
- ✔ *Old Master Portrait Drawings*, edited by Spero (or another collection of self-portraits)

My self-portrait shows the world how I see myself.

Setup

Instructional Sequence

1. Pass out mirrors and ask students to take a good look at themselves: eyes, mouth, hair, face shape, and so forth.

2. Show the class a book of self portraits by famous artists (such as *Old Master Portrait Drawings*).

3. Do a quick demonstration of how to draw a face (on the chalkboard or on a large piece of paper). Begin with an oval. Draw light lines to cut the oval into quarters. Draw almond-shaped eyes on the horizontal line. Draw the nose on the vertical line just below the horizontal line. Draw the ears outside the oval, at the horizontal line. Draw the mouth in the middle of the lower half of the oval. Add some hair. Show how to reshape the face to illustrate cheekbones, chin shape, and other features.

4. Hand out paper, pencils, and erasers. Explain that students should begin with a light sketch of their faces so they can easily erase mistakes.

5. Remind students to look at themselves often in the mirror to get ideas about the shapes (such as round, oval, or square) and colors (such as light tan, reddish, dark brown, or white with freckles) of and in their faces.

6. When students have finished their pencil drawings, hand out pastels or colored pencils so they can add colors. Groups can share these materials at each table.

7. Hang self-portraits on classroom or hallway walls.

Assessment

As you demonstrate and as students create, consider the following questions:

- Do students listen during whole group instruction and follow directions?

- Do students put care and effort into their drawings?

- If working at tables, do students cooperate with their tablemates for supplies?

- Do students demonstrate knowledge of art concepts, such as use of shapes and shading?

Wherever we go, whatever we do, self is the sole subject we study and learn.
—Ralph Waldo Emerson

Variations

- Students could draw one self-portrait per month and make a book at the end of the year.

- Students could bring in photographs of their faces. Enlarge the photographs on a copier (so the faces are 8 1/2 x 11). Have each student cut the copy of his or her face in half, glue one half to a white piece of construction paper, then draw the opposite half of the face.

- Students could sculpt busts of themselves out of clay.

- You could bring in several magazines with pictures of people and faces. Students cut out pieces of faces that resemble their own and glue them together on construction paper, creating a collage self-portrait. Alternatively, students could bring in family photographs. Enlarge the photographs on a copier so that students can cut out features from copies of family photographs to create self-portraits.

Songs from the Heart

Standards
(See pages 122–23.)

- Writing
- Communication
- Art

Guiding Concepts
(See pages viii–x.)

- Meaning making
- Emotion
- Self-reflection

Multiple Intelligences
(See page 124.)

- Verbal-linguistic
- Musical-rhythmic
- Intrapersonal
- Interpersonal

Goals

Students will share songs that are special to them in order to explore lessons and meaning in music and to share the feelings they experience.

Time

30 minutes per week (enough weeks for each student)

Grade Range

4–8

Materials

✔ song journals (make or buy)

✔ recording of a song that is special to you

✔ large piece of paper (at least 2 x 3 feet)

✔ pens or pencils

Setup

- Pick a song that is special to you, has good lessons, and evokes strong emotions. (See page 139 for song ideas.)

- Write the lyrics on the big piece of paper.

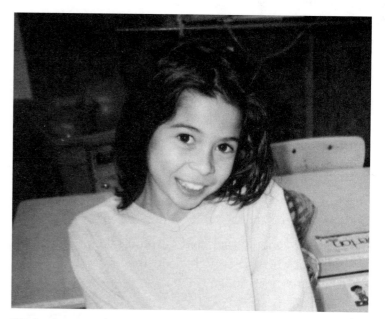

Music always makes me smile.

Instructional Sequence

1. Turn the lights down and ask the students to find a comfortable place to sit.

2. Play your song for them. Display the lyrics.

3. Ask students what they liked or disliked about the song. Ask comprehension questions such as "What do you think the singer was trying to say?" and "What did the song mean to you?"

4. Explain why the song is special to you. Talk about how music can comfort, inspire, calm, excite, and so forth. Discuss lyrics: how metaphors, word choice, word order, and so forth can convey meaning and evoke emotion. Discuss music: how tempo, instrument types, rhythm, and so forth can also convey meaning and evoke emotion.

5. Tell students they will each get a chance to share a song that is special to them. They will lead a class discussion about their songs, including what the songs mean to them, the emotions they evoke, the stylistic devices (such as metaphor, alliteration, rhyming) in the lyrics, the choice of instruments, the tempo and rhythm, and so forth. (Younger students can ask their parents or older siblings for help.) Give guidelines on appropriate language and content of songs.

6. Pass out song journals and ask students to write down their thoughts and feelings as you replay your song.

7. Every week, one student shares one song, accompanied by class discussion and journal writing.

Assessment

During your presentation and during student presentations, consider the following questions:

- Do students demonstrate listening and comprehension skills?

- Can students articulate their thoughts and feelings?

- Do students understand and apply music and language concepts when discussing songs?

Variations

- Students could write poems, paint pictures, or perform an interpretive dance or skit to retell each song.

- You could make a tape of everyone's special songs. Have a party after every student has shared a song and play the tape. Display art and writing projects if you include them as part of this activity (see previous variation).

- You could all vote on songs to learn as a class and give a concert.

- Students could compare different types of music (country, rock, classical, jazz, rap, folk, and so forth) or music from different cultures.

- Students could perform their favorite songs by singing them, playing an instrument, or giving a dramatic recitation of the lyrics.

More Art and Music Activity Ideas

- Students could try drawing with their feet to help them understand others' frustrations.

- Students could listen to music for particular mood effects (calming or energizing, for example).

- You could compile excerpts of songs that differ as greatly as possible, then play the compilation and have students draw what they feel as each song plays.

- Students could learn how to make up songs to help with memorization, such as to memorize the 50 states or the names of historical figures.

- On a field trip to a museum, or using Internet museums or art books, students could search for works of art that depict specific emotions, including joy, anger, grief, loneliness, excitement, love, apathy, and so on, then write brief summaries of each work. Students could follow this up by starting each day or week drawing, painting, or sculpting what they feel.

- You could teach rhythm and teamwork by having students choose ordinary objects in the classroom (such as pencils, boxes, trash cans, rubber bands, and so forth), then dividing them into groups in which each student has a different object. Teach each group a different rhythm, then bring all groups together to play as a rhythmic ensemble.

- If you have access to a video camera, students could create a music video of a favorite class song.

- Students could explore creative dance to different types of music, discussing and showing the ways emotions are expressed in dance.

Add your own ideas:

Chapter 4

Physical Activities

Gleaning

Standards
(See pages 122–23.)

- Communication
- Art
- Health and fitness

Guiding Concepts
(See pages viii–x.)

- Meaning making
- Character
- Connections
- Nature

Multiple Intelligences
(See page 124.)

- Bodily-kinesthetic
- Interpersonal
- Naturalist

Goals

- Students will contribute to their community in a positive way by donating their time and effort and by giving to people in need.
- Students will also work in groups and enjoy nature.

Time

6 hours over 2 days

Grade Range

2–8

Materials

- ✔ flyers (see Setup)
- ✔ paper grocery bags
- ✔ map of the neighborhood (if necessary)
- ✔ construction paper
- ✔ crayons, pastels, or colored markers

The gleaning activity takes children to the trees.

Setup

- Make a flyer to pass around the neighborhood that asks neighbors if they would like students to glean their fruit trees for them. The class will leave whatever good fruit the neighbors want, donate the rest to a local food bank, and compost the rotten fruit. Include a phone number for them to call and a date for gleaning. (You could ask students to draw pictures to put on the flyer.)

- Line up parent volunteers to accompany groups of students on two different days: one day when they pass out the flyers and another day when they glean the fruit. Your class could also pair with another class.

Instructional Sequence

1. Ask students to wear warm clothes the next day (if necessary) because they will be out in the community for an hour or so passing out flyers.

2. Tell them that on another day, they will be gleaning. Ask if anyone knows what that means.

3. Explain that *gleaning* is picking fruit from trees and off the ground when it is ripe. Explain what the class will be doing (as described in Setup).

4. The next day, divide students into groups of four or five and assign a parent and a section of the neighborhood to each group. Students will deliver flyers to each house in the neighborhood. Only one or two students should approach each house, so groups will need to work out a fair way to alternate delivery.

5. On gleaning day, at least one week after passing out the flyers, have a class discussion about respecting others, the yards, the trees, and so forth. Explain the procedure for gleaning. Students will pick and gather fruit into two bags (good fruit and rotten fruit). They should share duties with their classmates and behave responsibly (no climbing, throwing fruit, and so forth).

6. Hand out several bags to each group (so they have six for each house). Remind the group to use separate bags for good fruit and for rotten fruit. The adult volunteer should find out how much good fruit the neighbor wants to keep, then leave a bag (or more) of that fruit at the house.

7. Give the adult in each group addresses for the houses the group will visit. Gleaning will take at least one hour per house. The number of houses per group will depend on the size of your class and the response from the neighborhood.

8. When students return, separate the good fruit bags from the others. An adult can deliver the good fruit to the food bank. Students can compost the rotten fruit for a school garden. If your school does not have a garden, ask parents and other teachers if they compost at home, or ask your local nursery or orchard if they could use the fruit for compost.

9. Ask students to draw pictures and write one or two sentences on the pictures about what they did and what they learned. Display the pictures in the hall.

10. Have a discussion about charity and community service. Ask the students: "How did helping others make you feel? What are some other ways you could help others? Is it important to help others? Why?"

Assessment

Before, during, and after this activity, consider the following questions:

- Do students respect the neighbors, their group (including the adult), and the trees?

- Do students demonstrate an understanding of charity and community service?

- Do student pictures and sentences demonstrate that they learned from the experience?

Variations

- Students could collect berries or garden vegetables.

- Instead of gleaning, students could pick up and throw away or recycle litter in the neighborhood.

- You could send flyers around the neighborhood asking for clothing, household items, canned goods, or other donations a local shelter is seeking. Have children go around in groups collecting the items.

- Students could work in groups to plant trees or gardens in the community. (Note that gardens would require regular care throughout the year.)

- You could teach a unit on composting and gardening, planting a class garden and using the rotten fruit to compost the garden.

. . . that best portion of a good man's life,
His little, nameless, unremembered acts
Of kindness and of love.
—William Wordsworth

Popcorn Minute

Standards
(See pages 122–23.)

- Health and fitness

Guiding Concepts
(See pages viii–x.)

- Connections
- Self-reflection
- Emotion

Multiple Intelligences
(See page 124.)

- Bodily-kinesthetic
- Intrapersonal

Goals

- Students will learn how to be fully present in the moment.

- Students will learn to calm their bodies, minds, and spirits.

- Students will learn how to focus their thoughts on tasks and notice details they would normally overlook.

Time

5–15 minutes

Grade Range

K–8

Materials

- ✔ popcorn popper and popcorn (or buy prepopped corn)

- ✔ bowl

- ✔ soft mood music (optional—see page 141 for possible selections)

Setup

Pop some popcorn (enough for you and each student to have one piece) and put on soft music.

Instructional Sequence

1. Holding the bowl of popcorn, begin a discussion by asking students if any of them are really looking forward to something, if they have been thinking about something a lot.

2. Guide the conversation to arrive at the conclusion that many of us spend so much time in the future (thinking about things to come) or in the past (reminiscing about things gone by) that we miss the special moment we are in.

3. Explain that you will all do a quick activity that will help you and the students remember how to live in the moment and relax at the same time.

4. Ask students to take one piece of popcorn and hold it in their hands, but don't eat it yet.

5. Explain that they will take one minute to eat their pieces of popcorn. They can study them, smell them, nibble them, suck on them, feel them, and whatever else they think to do.

6. Explain that it is important that the one minute be silent. All students will spend that time with their own thoughts.

7. Ask students to notice what thoughts drift into their minds and then to focus their thoughts back on the popcorn.

8. Settle the class and begin the minute. Model how you can eat a piece of popcorn very slowly, noticing all the small details that you usually overlook, such as textures, colors, shapes, and tastes.

9. After the one minute, discuss what students thought about and noticed.

Assessment

During and after the activity, assess the following:

- Do students follow directions and spend the minute quietly?

- Do students seem more calm and relaxed after the exercise?

Variations

- You could use raisins or any other small piece of food.

- As students improve at focusing for one minute, you could increase the time.

- The class could use this exercise to calm down after recess or to focus before writing in journals or taking a test.

- Students could free-write about the experience of concentrating on the popcorn.

> *Silence is the absolute poise or balance of body, mind, and spirit.*
>
> —Ohiyesa

Shaking Energy

Standards
(See pages 122–23.)
- Health and fitness

Guiding Concepts
(See pages viii–x.)
- Emotion
- Self-reflection

Multiple Intelligences
(See page 124.)
- Bodily-kinesthetic
- Intrapersonal

Goals

- Students will be aware of their bodies and emotions.
- Students will learn a tool to release bottled-up anxiety and nervous energy.

Time

5–15 minutes

Grade Range

K–8

Materials

✔ journals and pens or pencils (optional)

Setup

Instructional Sequence

1. After recess or physical education class, before a big test, or any other time when students need to calm down, ask them to stand up and come to the center of the room (or go outside).

2. Tell students to close their eyes and pay attention to their emotions and how their bodies feel. For example, they might notice how fast or slow their breathing is, whether certain muscles feel tired or tight, and what they are thinking about.

Feeling calm after shaking the energy.

3. Tell them to imagine that a warm, calm feeling is starting at the center of their bodies and pushing the anxiety, nervousness, or fidgety energy toward their fingers, toes, and head.

4. Have students shake their hands and imagine that the energy is leaving their fingertips and floating into the sky. Do the same with each foot.

5. Then tell students to shake their whole bodies to get out any other nervous energy that is hiding.

6. Ask students to stop shaking after a few minutes and take a moment to check in with their bodies and emotions again.

7. Remind them that they can do this on their own at appropriate times when they feel angry, nervous, or uneasy in any way.

8. Remind students that their bodies can tell them important things, and they should always try to listen to them. If they pay attention to their bodies, they may notice patterns in how they feel when they eat certain foods or how certain kinds of music or activities help them feel good inside.

9. Have discussions or journal time periodically about what they have learned from their bodies.

Assessment

During and after the activity, assess the following:

- Do students follow directions?

- Do students demonstrate through discussion and journal entries that they tuned in to their bodies?

Variations

- Students could do this activity without the visualization part. Just demonstrate how they can shake their arms and legs. The physical actions will help them relax.

- The class could try other physical relaxation exercises throughout the year, such as yoga or other stretching and breathing exercises.

- Students could write before-and-after journal entries, describing how they feel physically and emotionally before and after shaking energy.

More Physical Activity Ideas _____

- Try combining math and physical activity with a "cross-country" walk. Measure a distance at school, such as around the schoolyard or a track or someplace similar where students can walk regularly. Then have students choose where they wish to walk in the country. Put up a map of the United States. Each time the class walks the measured distance (around the schoolyard, track, or other), mark on the map how much closer to their destinations the students walked (using thumbtacks or markers). Students could study their destinations as they travel toward them.

- Students could role-play problems by taking the side opposite their own in a situation (putting themselves in someone else's shoes).

- You could lead students in creating a human knot: All students but one stand in a line holding hands (while the one student left out leaves the room). The first person in line then dips under the clasped hands of two students at any point in the line. The first person continues to dip under clasped hands, with the rest following (not letting go of hands) until the entire group is in a knot. The one student who left the room now comes back to untie the knot, again without any students letting go of hands.

- Students could spell out new vocabulary words using physical interpretation to create the letters (as a cheerleader would). Alternatively, students could act out the meaning of new vocabulary groups in a game of vocabulary charades.

- The class could start each day with stretching and breathing exercises.

- With partners, students could try to mirror each other's movements. One student leads while the other follows, then they swap. Students should do this as slowly as possible in the beginning.

- In small groups, students could learn dances from different cultures and then perform them for the class.

- Students could choose poems that are meaningful to them to act out for the class.

Add your own ideas:

Chapter 5

Social Studies Activities

Media Awareness

Standards
(See pages 122–23.)

- Writing
- Social studies
- Art

Guiding Concepts
(See pages viii–x.)

- Meaning making
- Emotion
- Connections

Multiple Intelligences
(See page 124.)

- Verbal-linguistic

Goals

- Students will become aware of the messages on television (particularly negative messages).
- Students will learn how to make conscious choices based on critical thought.

Time

2–3 hours, plus homework time

Grade Range

4–8

Materials

- ✔ journals (make or buy)
- ✔ sheet of paper large enough to cover a wall (as a backdrop for student work)
- ✔ art supplies (pastels, paints, markers, construction paper, poster paper, colored pencils, or anything you have on hand)
- ✔ video of the Road Runner and Wile E. Coyote, *The Three Stooges,* or some other show with obvious violence.

Setup

Cover a wall with paper labeled "What We See on TV."

Nurture awareness.

Instructional Sequence

1. Show the video and have a class discussion about the piece. What did students notice (humor, violence, and so forth)? What do they think other people might notice? Do they think TV influences people's behaviors and moods? Do they think watching TV is beneficial or harmful?

2. Explain that they will each take home their journals. As they are watching TV in the evenings, they will write down what they notice. (Students might want to videotape the shows, if they can, so they can review portions as needed.) They will look in particular for messages or behaviors portrayed in television shows: for example, violence solves problems, money is important, pretty people have more fun, and so forth. They should also write down any emotions that they have as they watch different shows.

3. Ask students to write down quotations from the TV characters or personalities whose words particularly stand out to them.

4. When students have gathered a week's worth of information (seven hours of TV), ask them to bring their journals back to school.

5. Explain that they will write papers (length appropriate to age) that describe what they observed, their opinions about what they observed, what the characters might have felt in the situations depicted in the shows, and what impact they think TV has on people in general.

6. Students will also make art pieces to hang on the paper backdrop you set up on the wall. The pieces can include drawings, quotes, emotions evoked, thoughts about TV, or anything else they believe is relevant.

7. Have a class discussion at the end of the project. Do students notice things they didn't notice before? Did their ideas about TV change? Do they think TV is an accurate representation of today's society? If so, do they like what they see? If not, why not?

Assessment

Throughout discussion and after the activity is completed, consider the following questions:

- Do students take good notes (detailed, with a focus on what's important) in their journals?

- Do students use critical-thinking skills to evaluate what they see on TV?

- Are students able to empathize with the characters?

- Do students use the writing process (prewriting, drafting, revising, editing, publishing) and develop the writing traits (ideas, organization, voice, word choice, sentence fluency, conventions, presentation) in their papers?

Variations

- Students could examine TV commercials; newspaper, magazine, and radio advertisements; video games; movies; or musical lyrics instead of television shows. They would consider the same issues: effect on behavior and mood; portrayal of subject matter; use of humor, violence, and so on; and whether what they see or hear reflects society.

- Students could create a script for a television show that avoids the negative elements they saw in other shows.

- You could extend the activity throughout the quarter, semester, or year: Students write in their journals each week, with class discussion every week or two. Evaluate journals to see if students fine-tune critical-thinking skills after each class discussion.

No one outside of ourselves can rule us inwardly. When we know this, we become free.

—Jack Kornfield

Future Places

Standards
(See pages 122–23.)

- Writing
- Communication
- Science
- Social studies
- Art

Guiding Concepts
(See pages viii–x.)

- Meaning making
- Intuitive knowing
- Creativity
- Connections

Multiple Intelligences
(See page 124.)

- Verbal-linguistic
- Logical-mathematical
- Visual-spatial
- Bodily-kinesthetic
- Interpersonal

Goals

- Students will imagine, create a model of, and write about a place in the future, incorporating government, education, environment, culture, and other aspects of society.

- Students will think of ways they can improve the world.

Time

1 hour for introduction; 3–6 hours of class time to create and work on written piece and model; 5–10 minutes of presentation time per student pair; and 2–4 hours' homework time

Grade Range

4–8

Materials

- ✔ a large piece of cardboard or wood for each pair of students (2 $\frac{1}{2}$ x 2 $\frac{1}{2}$ feet)

- ✔ miscellaneous art supplies, such as paints, glue, cups, craft sticks, toothpicks, boxes, and so forth

- ✔ paper and pens or pencils

Setup

- Decide requirements for the model and paper: For example, you might require description and demonstration of transportation, energy sources, economy, setting, people, government, and so forth. (You could create handouts that detail these requirements for students.)

- Collect books, videos, and magazines about the future for reference. Check with your school librarian for ideas or see the suggestions in Appendix C (on page 137). You local science museum may also have materials on loan.

Children will make a better future.

Instructional Sequence

1. Start a class discussion about the future by asking students, "What do you think the world will be like in 200 years?" List ideas as the class brainstorms. Ask questions as needed to guide students to think about business, environment, culture, transportation, education, religion, and so forth.

2. Explain that students will work with partners to create models of future places. These places can be anywhere in the world and of any type (city, farm, suburb, and so forth). They will also write individual papers (length is age dependent) describing their future places. Hand out or describe the paper and model requirements.

3. Tell students to ask themselves, "What would I do to improve the world?" These ideas will be part of their future models.

4. Ask students to choose partners (or choose for them prior to class) and ask partners to brainstorm together about their future places.

5. Give students class time to work on their models and papers. Set out all art supplies and give each pair a piece of wood or cardboard on which to build. The students can also work on their projects as homework.

6. Students present their future places to the class to wrap up the project. Presentations should include a brief description of their place's government, transportation, education system, and so forth, as well as their ideas to improve the world.

7. Revisit the list that students generated at the beginning of the activity. Did any of their ideas change?

8. Make a list of how the students will improve the world to display in the hall or classroom.

Assessment

Consider the following questions throughout the project:

- Do students participate in class discussions?

- Do students use creativity and teamwork to plan and build their future models?

- Do the models and papers include all of the required elements?

- Do students demonstrate understanding of interconnection of all aspects of their future setting (cause and effect)?

- Do students use the writing process (prewriting, drafting, revising, editing, publishing) in their written pieces?

- How well do students use the writing traits (ideas, organization, voice, word choice, sentence fluency, conventions, presentation) in their written pieces?

- Do students communicate their ideas effectively using artistic and verbal skills?

Variations

- You might have a future day or future party to wrap up the project. Students could dress up and decorate the classroom futuristically; listen to what they see as the music of the future; and bring in what they think will be the foods of the future (such as powdered ice cream).

- The class could visit a museum (on the Internet or in person) with an exhibit on the future.

- You might suggest an extra credit project: Students could read others' predictions about the future (such as those in science fiction) and write a paper about the ideas and whether they think the ideas are plausible.

- The class could display all projects with written abstracts and invite other classes to tour the future.

The only way to predict the future is to have power to shape the future.

—Eric Hoffer

America's First People

Standards
(See pages 122–23.)
- Reading
- Writing
- Social studies

Guiding Concepts
(See pages viii–x.)
- Meaning making
- Intuitive knowing
- Religion (objective study)
- Connections

Multiple Intelligences
(See page 124.)
- Verbal-linguistic
- Visual-spatial
- Interpersonal

Goals
- Students will learn about other cultures and correct their own misconceptions.
- Students will learn how many Native Americans find the sacred in life.

Time

2 hours for initial activity; 30 minutes per day throughout the week for additional stories; 5 minutes per student for presentations

Grade Range

1–6

Materials
- ✔ several books on Native Americans (see page 140 for suggestions), some for you to read, others for students to read individually or in small groups
- ✔ information chart (see page 126)
- ✔ index cards
- ✔ pens or pencils
- ✔ bulletin board (with tacks)
- ✔ construction paper and crayons or pastels (optional)

Setup
- Make copies of the information chart for students (the number of copies depends on how many tribes each student will study).
- Choose a book about Native Americans to read to the class when you introduce the lesson. You could start with a book about a tribe native to your region. The book can be either nonfiction or fiction that realistically portrays Native American culture.
- Prepare a blank bulletin board with "We learned that . . ." across the top.

Instructional Sequence

1. Ask students what they know about Native Americans. (Write down all answers.)

2. Ask students what they would like to learn about Native Americans. (Write down these answers too.)

3. Read a book about Native Americans, perhaps from a tribe native to your region.

4. Lay out several other books for students to read on their own or in small groups, and

pass out the information charts so they can record their information. Ask students to write their favorite interesting facts on index cards and pin them on the bulletin board. They could also draw pictures about what they learn to add to the board.

5. Read one fictional book about Native Americans each day of the week. Have a class discussion about the accuracy of the stories. Are Native Americans portrayed realistically based on students' research?

6. For homework, ask students to do a project that shows what they have learned, such as a poem, story, shoe box setting (diorama), or painting.

7. Have students share their projects with the class to teach others what they discovered.

8. Revisit the list that students generated at the beginning of the activity. Did any of their ideas about Native Americans change?

Assessment

Throughout the research, discussion, and presentations, consider the following questions:

- Do students demonstrate research and comprehension skills?

- Do student presentations show acquired knowledge about Native Americans?

- Do students use critical-thinking skills to reevaluate their ideas about other cultures?

- Do students show respect for other cultures?

Variations

- If you have Native American students, you could ask them to share stories about their cultures and family histories.

- The class could go on a field trip to a place that teaches about Native Americans from your region, such as a museum, cultural center, or Native American reservation.

- You could invite a Native American guest speaker to talk about his or her culture.

- You could show videos about Native American culture and history. (See page 136 for suggestions.)

- You could adapt the activity to cover another ethnic group.

Humankind has not woven the web of life. We are but one thread within it. Whatever we do to the web, we do to ourselves. All things are bound together. All things connect.

—Chief Seattle

More Social Studies Activity Ideas _____

- The class could have a day in the life of a school in 1776 (emulate a one-room schoolhouse, dress up, use quill pens, bring bucket lunches, play games of the time, and so forth).

- Throughout the year, students could write journal entries or autobiographies from the perspectives of people they are studying.

- At the beginning of the year, you could assess the multiple intelligences in your students, then pair up students with different strengths and weaknesses to be study partners for the year. Allow time periodically (such as before tests) for partners to work together in class.

- Throughout history units, students could study the most creative people in the given period, including personality traits, personal beliefs, the multiple intelligences of the people, biographical information, achievements, obstacles, and so forth.

- Throughout history units, you could enhance students' intuitive thinking by always asking if they can guess what happens next before telling them.

- Students could write self-reflective pieces about current events throughout the year. For example, they might write about how current events affect them as well as write from the perspective of other people who appear in news stories (such as those in another country during war).

- Students could work in groups to study prominent Americans from various ethnic and cultural backgrounds. One group might study Asian Americans; another might study African Americans; another might study Native Americans; and so forth. Students could write biographical sketches; draw or paint portraits; write and perform plays; hold mock debates; impersonate the famous people; and so forth.

- Students could study the origin of holidays around the world.

- Students could research historical events and write papers on what society can learn from them.

Add your own ideas:

Chapter 6

Community and Connections Activities

Kindness Tree _____

Standards
(See pages 122–23.)

- Reading
- Writing
- Communication

Guiding Concepts
(See pages viii–x.)

- Character
- Emotion
- Connections

Multiple Intelligences
(See page 124.)

- Verbal-linguistic
- Visual-spatial
- Interpersonal

Goals

- Students will notice and appreciate kind acts throughout the day.
- Students will strive to be kind to others.

Time

10–15 minutes

Grade Range

K–4

Materials

- ✔ big tree (made with paper or other material) without leaves on a wall or bulletin board
- ✔ pieces of green paper (or fall colors) cut into leaf shapes
- ✔ tape or stapler

Setup

- Label the wall or board "Kindness Tree."
- Keep the stack of paper leaves near the tree.

Instructional Sequence

1. Throughout the day, look for students who are kind to others. Say to them, "The way you _____ was so kind. I think that needs to go on the kindness tree." Then write the student names on the leaves, along with details of their kind acts. Tape or staple leaves to the branches on the tree. Students will begin to realize the purpose of the tree.

This is my friend.

2. At the end of the day, ask a student to go to the tree and read one of the leaves to the class. Ask everyone to thank the person described on the leaf.

3. Explain that there were many other kind acts throughout the day and point to the remaining leaves as evidence. Ask the students to thank each other for the kind things they remember. Demonstrate: "Thank you, Steven, for helping me clean up the blocks."

4. After students catch on to the idea of the kindness tree, explain that they can add kindness leaves to the tree themselves. They must be specific and detailed about the act of kindness they wish to recognize. Encourage younger students to get help with writing from other students, teachers, and parent volunteers.

5. Routinely choose leaves to read (once a day, once a week, or as often as you wish), recognize the act of kindness, and thank each other for other acts.

6. Talk about how kindness grows like the leaves on the tree.

Assessment

Keep the following questions in mind throughout the life of the kindness tree:

- Do students begin to act more kindly to each other?

- Do all students add leaves to the tree?

- Do students thank each other during the day for acts of kindness?

Variations

- You could read books with kindness themes (or have students read them). (See page 138 for suggestions.)

- Students could complete journal entries as homework (or in class). Entry assignments might include writing about the kindnesses of others in their lives outside of school; the differences among being kind to friends, family, strangers, and people we don't like; and community service as an act of kindness.

- Students could write a story or poem about what the world would be like if everyone tried to be kind to one another.

- You could use a different form besides a tree, such as stars in the sky, balloons floating around the room, or flowers in big paper vases on the walls.

Pen Pals

Standards
(See pages 122–23.)

- Reading
- Writing
- Social Studies

Guiding Concepts
(See pages viii–x.)

- Meaning making
- Connections

Multiple Intelligences
(See page 124.)

- Verbal-linguistic
- Interpersonal

Goals

Students will learn about other cultures and make new friends through writing and reading letters.

Time

1–2 hours per letter, 3–4 times during the year

Grade Range

2–8

Materials

- ✔ globe
- ✔ paper
- ✔ pencils or pens
- ✔ envelopes
- ✔ camera
- ✔ film

Setup

Find a school in another state or country that would like to participate. (Try searching the Internet for pen pals. See page 139 for suggested websites.)

Instructional Sequence

1. Gather children around you and a globe. Show on the globe where you are, point to where their pen pals live, and ask if anyone knows anything about the town, country, or culture of their pen pals.

2. Ask students what they would like to know about the town, country, and culture. Make a list on the board.

Students learn about each other through letters.

3. Explain that they will each have a pen pal from this place. Give them some information about the school, the pen pal process (that is, that pen pals write letters back and forth to learn about each other, and that it may take some time for the letters to arrive), and so forth.

4. Talk about the format of a letter, such as date, greeting, body, closing, and signature. For older children, you could discuss the difference between a business letter and a personal letter (such as the former being more formal and including addresses and titles).

5. Brainstorm information that students might want to put in their letters about themselves, such as interests, age, family, favorite school activities, and so forth.

6. Ask students to get out a piece of paper and write a letter to a pen pal. (Students may have to write a generic "Dear Pen Pal" for the first letter. Students on the other end will choose a letter and write back to a specific student.)

7. While the students are working on their letters, take a picture of each student to include in the letters.

8. Help students edit their letters for spelling and grammar. Some students may need guidance for content as well.

9. After the pictures have been developed, have students put their letters and pictures in an envelope.

10. Put all the envelopes in a large envelope and mail it to the teacher of the pen pal class.

11. When pen pals return letters, give students time to read the letters and share them with their classmates. What are their pen pals' names? What did they learn from them? What do they want to write about next?

12. Give students time to write back to their pen pals. Discuss responding to any questions their pen pals asked, asking more questions, and including something new about themselves.

Assessment

Consider the following questions as students write letters:

- Do students put care and thought into their letters?

- Do students use editing skills to correct letters?

As students discuss the letters from their pen pals, consider the following questions:

- Do students learn from their pen pals?

- Do students make connections and notice similarities between themselves and their pen pals?

Variations

- Students could correspond with pen pals via e-mail.
- You could send a videotape of students introducing themselves.
- Older students might be able to visit the pen pal school.
- You could choose a pen pal school on a Native American reservation in your state and visit the school at the end of the year. Coordinate with the other teacher on cultural greetings and hospitality.

Our chief want in life is somebody who shall make us do what we can; this is the service of a friend.
—Ralph Waldo Emerson

Positive Thoughts

Standards

(See pages 122–23.)

- Communication

Guiding Concepts

(See pages viii–x.)

- Emotion
- Creativity
- Connections
- Self-reflection

Multiple Intelligences

(See page 124.)

- Verbal-linguistic
- Intrapersonal
- Interpersonal

Goals

- Students will become aware of their thoughts and reactions to events in their lives.

- Students will begin to make a conscious choice to think and act positively toward themselves and others.

Time

15–20 minutes

Grade Range

K–8

Materials

Setup

Choose an event to present to the class, an event that would affect students, such as a fight among students, a teacher leaving the school suddenly, the death of someone close to a student or teacher, a student who is ill, or more general topics such as what it's like to be picked on or what it feels like to be good at something and not so good at something.

Think happy.

Instructional Sequence

1. Describe an event that would affect students in the class. The event could be fictitious or something that has happened in class or in the school.

2. Ask students to share their thoughts about the event. Each time a student shares a thought, ask if it is a negative thought or a positive thought. Ask how it makes him or her feel physically.

3. Ask students if they can change their negative thoughts to positive thoughts. For example, if a student is thinking that the death of a grandparent is sad, the positive thought would be to think of what in the life of that grandparent was happy. What would the positive alternatives to their negative thoughts be and how does the positive thought change the way they feel physically?

4. Discuss the idea that thinking positively can have a positive effect on people. They think differently, feel differently, and therefore act differently. For instance, if you think you will do well on a test, rather than assuming you will do poorly, you will be less anxious, which may result in a better outcome. Similarly, if you expect people to be friendly, you will approach them more openly. They will often respond by being more open and friendly with you.

5. Ask everyone to sit quietly for a few minutes and think of a positive thought for the day. It could be as simple as "I will have a good day" or "I will do well on my test." Have students repeat their positive thoughts to themselves and notice their emotions and how their bodies feel.

6. Tell students that they can also send positive thoughts to others. If someone is sick or sad, come up with a positive thought as a class and sit quietly for a few minutes sending the thought to the person.

7. Try this activity each morning to focus or use it as a problem-solving technique.

Assessment

As the class practices positive thinking, note whether they begin to approach events and problems in positive ways.

Variations

- Discuss how thinking and action can go hand in hand by suggesting ways to help a sick or sad person, such as making a get well card or singing a funny song to cheer a person up.

- The class can try to send positive thoughts to a group of needy people, such as the homeless or the terminally ill. Follow up with positive action, such as collecting blankets or food for the homeless or visiting a hospice.

- You could work on positive thinking with students on an individual basis. Some students may open up more about their thoughts if they aren't sharing with the class.

- Students could keep a journal of negative thoughts to help them recognize negative thinking throughout their day. Next to each negative thought, they should write a positive alternative.

For you are the creator of your reality, and life can show up no other way for you than that way in which you think it will.

—Neale Donald Walsch

Talking Circle _____

Standards
(See pages 122–23.)
- Communication

Guiding Concepts
(See pages viii–x.)
- Connections
- Self-reflection

Multiple Intelligences
(See page 124.)
- Verbal-linguistic
- Interpersonal

Goals

- Students will create a community by sharing special moments with their classmates.
- Students will practice listening skills and speaking to a group of people.

Time

15–20 minutes

Grade Range

K–8

Materials

✔ a class totem of some kind: a decorated stick (*talking stick*) or some other item to pass around a circle (At the beginning of the year, the class can make a talking stick as a way to create community.)

Setup

Learn more about talking stick traditions and how to create a talking stick. (See the suggested reading on page 139.)

Instructional Sequence

1. Gather students in a circle (either sitting on the floor or in a circle of tables, desks, or chairs). Tell students that the talking circle is a time for each person to share something special. They might share news about their families (such as a new little brother or sister), something fun they did over the weekend (such as a camping trip), or an achievement or activity they are particularly proud of (such as winning a soccer game or learning how to do something new).

2. Go over the rules of a talking circle: Only the person holding the talking stick may talk. Others should be actively listening. *Active listening* means they are not thinking about what they will say or what they will be doing later. They should be really listening to the person who is talking.

3. The circle goes clockwise and everyone gets a chance to talk if they choose. They have the option to pass.

4. Have a talking circle one or two times a week: Monday morning talking circles work well because students often have things from the weekend to share.

Assessment

During each talking circle and throughout the year, consider the following questions:

- Do students listen to others and are they respectful of other people's comments?

- Do students share stories? (The talking circle can identify those children who are uncomfortable talking to groups of people.)

- Does the classroom community grow stronger as the year progresses?

Variations

- For young students, you could split the group in two so the time sitting is shorter (or do half one day and the other half the other day).

- Talking circles are a nice way to close an adult staff meeting or retreat.

- You could use a talking circle on the first day of class as a way for students to introduce themselves and get to know each other.

- The class could use a talking circle after a field trip for students to share their different perspectives and experiences.

If someone listens, or stretches out a hand, or whispers a kind word of encouragement, or attempts to understand a lonely person, extraordinary things begin to happen.

—Loretta Gizartis

Trust Walk

Standards
(See pages 122–23.)
- Communication

Guiding Concepts
(See pages viii–x.)
- Intuitive knowing
- Connections
- Character

Multiple Intelligences
(See page 124.)
- Bodily-kinesthetic
- Interpersonal

Goals

- Students will learn about trusting other people and trusting their own feelings (intuition).
- Students will experience being responsible for another person.

Time

1–2 hours

Grade Range

2–8

Materials

✔ blindfolds

✔ craft sticks (optional)

✔ journals (optional)

Setup

Find a good open place where students can do the trust walk. If the weather is nice, do it outdoors.

Instructional Sequence

1. Gather students together and ask, "What is trust?"

2. Guide discussion about trust: Why is it important? How can it improve our lives? Introduce the idea of trusting yourself—your own ideas, feelings, and thoughts (your *intuition*).

3. Assign partners by pulling out craft sticks with students' names on them from a box or other container, or assign partners in some other random way.

4. Explain that each student will take turns being the guide while the other partner is blindfolded.

5. Ask students for ideas about how the guide should behave and what the guide's responsibilities are. (A guide is responsible for another person's safety and feelings. They should treat their partners the way they want to be treated.)

6. Take students to the area where the trust walk will take place and give each set of partners one blindfold.

7. Explain that each student will have 15 minutes as the guide. Explain the boundaries of the area in which they will walk and any other rules. This might be a good time to remind students to be safe, take the activity seriously, and be respectful to each other.

8. Ask one member of each group to put on the blindfold. Start timing and tell the guides to begin the trust walk anywhere in the defined area.

9. After 15 minutes, ask partners to switch roles.

10. Have a debriefing discussion or a journal writing session (or both) about how it felt to be the guide and to be the one who was trusting the guide. How can this translate to life? For example, being trusted and being able to trust someone feels good. Trust is an important part of relationships, school and work, self-esteem, and so forth.

Assessment

Before, during, and after this activity, assess student attitude and understanding:

- Do students take the role of guide seriously and act responsibly?

- Do students use critical-thinking skills to consider the idea of trust (as shown in discussion or journals)?

Variations

- The class could try a trust fall: In groups of four to six students, one student stands in the middle with eyes closed (or blindfolded). The others are in a close circle around the student. The middle student lets his or her body fall in different directions. The circle of students gently pushes the middle student back to the center. Discuss balance and trust, such as how people you trust can help you through difficult (unbalanced) times in your life.

- The class could try a trust taste: Pair up students, as with the trust walk, but this time guides give the blindfolded person different food items so he or she can explore the senses of touch, smell, taste, and sound.

- Students could write journal entries about or discuss with the class times they have trusted or not trusted themselves.

> *When you trust in yourself, you trust in the wisdom that created you.*
>
> —Dr. Wayne Dyer

Word Tools

Standards
(See pages 122–23.)
- Communication

Guiding Concepts
(See pages viii–x.)
- Meaning making
- Character
- Emotion

Multiple Intelligences
(See page 124.)
- Verbal-linguistic
- Interpersonal

Goals

- Students will respond to problematic social situations using words instead of violence.
- Students will learn to express themselves clearly.
- Students will increase their vocabularies.

Time

20–30 minutes

Grade Range

K–2

Setup

Observe daily classroom dynamics and problems that come up over and over again between children. Choose a list of words that apply to the situations you observe, such as "threat," "bully," "cheating," and "teasing."

Instructional Sequence

1. Bring up one of the words during a class meeting. For example, "Does anyone know what a threat is?" Listen to students' ideas about the word you introduce. Add your own ideas if needed.

2. Explain that people can use their words as tools when someone threatens them. For example, they can say, "Stop. You can't do that. That's a threat."

3. Have children repeat these words with you.

4. Ask questions to test understanding. For example, "What if someone says that he's going to hit you if you don't let him play?"

5. Use this activity to explore other issues in the classroom throughout the year.

Assessment

Throughout the school year, observe students' word choices:

- Do students start using their word tools during the school day to solve problems?

- Do students use their new vocabulary in their writing?

- Do students recognize the new words in their reading?

Variations

- You could introduce a word and action by reading a book to the class that includes that word and action. (See suggestions on page 139.)

- You could put up a large sheet of paper where students can add words they would like to discuss. As problems come up during the day, you could suggest that they put words related to the problems on the "Word Tools" list.

- Students could practice how to ask for what they want. For instance, to say "I want you to be nicer" does not define how you want a person to act. Explain to students that we need to tell people *how* they could be nicer. For example: "I want you to stop throwing blocks at me when you get upset. Will you do that?"

- Students could brainstorm words to describe their feelings, then discuss when to use these words.

No one can make you feel inferior without your consent.

—Eleanor Roosevelt

More Community and Connections Activity Ideas

- You could conduct a student interest survey and choose activities based on the results.

- The class could have regular class meetings. When students have problems in the classroom (with classmates or rules), they add their name to the class meeting list. During the class meeting, students from the list explain their problems and classmates offer solutions. The student with the problem chooses one to try. You act as a facilitator and give solutions only when students can't think of any. At your discretion, you may decide a problem requires adult intervention, at which point you would need to talk to the student privately rather than sharing the problem with the class. (See *Positive Discipline,* by Jane Nelsen, for more details on class meetings.)

- Students could study their local communities in depth: using their senses (what do students see, smell, taste, hear, and touch in the community); studying the history; studying and getting involved in local government; discussing their connections with the community; studying the overall cultural makeup of the community; discussing what they like and don't like, and how to make changes; learning about the area's natural resources and how they are used; and so forth.

- Students could create their own rules for the classroom. Include discussion about why rules are necessary, which rules are easier or more difficult to follow than others and why, what happens when we don't follow rules, and so forth.

- Students could investigate activism, including causes for activism, effects of activism, famous activist organizations, and causes for student activism.

- The class could learn about our interdependence on the rest of the world by studying the origins of food and other goods we use regularly. You might begin by asking students to examine tags on clothing to determine where the clothing was made, then encourage them to study the origins of other goods, such as cars, building materials, food, and so forth. They could then study the countries from which the goods originate.

- Students could work in small groups throughout the year for problem-solving activities such as riddles, word problems, physical activities that require teamwork (such as building a bridge or tower out of miscellaneous materials), decision-making (working in groups to discuss all possible options in hypothetical scenarios), and so forth.

Add your own ideas:

Chapter 7

Thematic Units

All about Me

Standards
(See pages 122–23.)

- Writing
- Art
- Communication

Guiding Concepts
(See pages viii–x.)

- Meaning making
- Emotion
- Creativity
- Self-reflection

Multiple Intelligences
(See page 124.)

- Verbal-linguistic
- Visual-spatial
- Intrapersonal

About This Unit

For this unit, students ask questions to get to know themselves and answer those questions through the following writing and art activities:

1. Cover Art (30 to 45 minutes)
2. The Color Most Like My Mood (30 to 45 minutes)
3. I Like the Feel Of . . . (30 to 45 minutes)
4. I Like the Taste Of . . . (30 to 45 minutes)
5. I Like the Sound Of . . . (30 to 45 minutes)
6. I Like the Smell Of . . . (30 to 45 minutes)
7. I Hope (30 to 45 minutes)

Goals

- Students will develop intra-personal skills: They will learn about themselves and what is important to them.
- Students will communicate effectively using writing and art.

Time

30–40 minutes per day for 7 days

Grade Range

1–4

When I get to know others, I get to know myself.

Assessment for This Unit

Keep the following questions in mind through-out this unit. See individual activities for more specific assessment ideas.

- Do students express thoughts effectively through writing and art?

- Do students follow directions?

- Do students show growth from the previous grade: Do they use new words, interesting examples, expanded word definitions (of hope, feelings, senses, and so forth)?

- Do students finish the book?

Unit Variations

- This unit is obviously geared toward younger children. For older students, you could use abstract ideas—fear, wonder, belief, desire, regret, and so on—instead of the five senses. Students could write paragraphs about each concept. The first line would be a statement (such as "I regret . . ."); the rest of the paragraph would explain why they have the regret and perhaps how they could avoid regret in the future. Older students might work on more involved art projects, such as abstract art that expresses ideas through metaphor, using charcoal, pastels, or oil paints.

- You could read (or have students read) books to accompany activities three through seven. (See page 136 for suggested reading.)

We carry within us the wonders we seek without us.
—Sir Thomas Browne

Activity 1

Cover Art

About This Activity

This first activity kicks off the All about Me unit with an art project to help students express themselves visually as they focus on who they are.

Materials

✔ two 8 ¹/₂ x 11 pieces of poster board for each student

✔ crayons

✔ pastels

✔ pencils

✔ binding material (such as a binding machine, yarn and a hole punch, or a stapler)

✔ prewritten pages (on pages 127–32)

✔ laminator (optional)

Setup

■ Prepare poster board: Each student needs two 8 ¹/₂ x 11 pieces to use as front and back covers.

■ Photocopy or re-create prewritten pages.

Instructional Sequence

1. Explain to students that they are going to make special books. They are special because they are books about them that they can keep for their whole lives.

2. Explain that students can decorate the covers of their special books with any drawings and words they choose. Their names should be on the covers somewhere.

3. Allow time for students to decorate their covers.

4. Laminate the decorated cover (optional) and bind it with the other poster board piece as the back cover, with prewritten pages between.

Assessment

Consider student comprehension and effort during this activity:

■ Do students include their names on their covers, as directed?

■ Do students put thought and effort into decorating their covers?

■ Do students show understanding that these covers are part of a book they will create about themselves?

Variations

• Students could decorate both front and back covers.

• Students could do the cover art last, after the other activities. Bind the books after students have completed the contents.

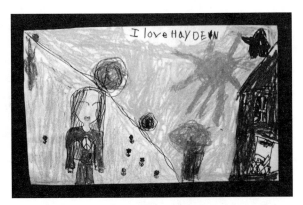

A student uses art and words to describe emotion.

— Activity 2 —

The Color Most Like My Mood

About This Activity

This second activity of the All about Me unit encourages children to understand themselves, particularly their moods and feelings, using color as a metaphor.

Materials

- ✔ first page of book (See page 127.)
- ✔ half sheets of white construction paper
- ✔ tempera paints: red, yellow, blue, black, and white
- ✔ glue stick
- ✔ *My Many Colored Days,* by Dr. Seuss, or *Hailstones and Halibut Bones,* by O'Neill and Wallner (or both books)

Setup

Instructional Sequence

1. Read *My Many Colored Days* or *Hailstones and Halibut Bones* (or both). Begin a discussion about how a color can represent a feeling or a mood. A person could feel like a different color on a different day. Each person will define each color differently: For example, purple may represent sadness to one person and happiness to another.

2. Explain that students will work on the first page of their books. Read aloud the sentence at the top of the page: "My mood today is like the color _____ because _____."

3. Remind students that this is not a sentence about their favorite colors but a sentence about the colors that represent how they are feeling today.

4. Brainstorm with students about what they can write for the first page. Explain that they should write on only the top half of the page because they will be adding an art project to the other half.

5. Explain that after the students write their sentences, they will paint pictures that represent their feelings for the day, including the colors they chose. They will get black and white paint, as well as red, yellow, and blue paints to mix, if necessary. Lead a mini-discussion about primary colors. ("Why did I choose these three colors?" and "How do you make purple, green, and orange?")

6. After the paintings dry, have students glue them onto page 1 of their books with a glue stick.

My mood today is like the color yellow because yellow is a smiley sun and a sweet-smelling flower.

81

The Color Most Like My Mood

Assessment

Throughout this activity, assess student comprehension and effort:

- Do students understand the difference between a favorite color and a color that represents a feeling or mood?

- Do students put thought and effort into describing their feeling or mood in writing and in their paintings?

Variations

- Students could use other materials to create their art, such as pastels, crayons, or colored pencils.

- Older students could write a short story or poem using color to indicate various moods and feelings.

- The class could also study paintings and discuss whether the artist used color to reflect his or her mood when working on the painting.

The highest and most profitable reading is the true knowledge and consideration of ourselves.

—Thomas A. Kempis

--- **Activity 3** ---

I Like the Feel Of . . .

About This Activity

This third activity of the All about Me unit encourages children to think about all five senses, then to focus on the sense of touch and how what they enjoy touching can reflect who they are.

Materials

✔ second page of book (See page 128.)

✔ crayons

✔ pastels

✔ fabric

✔ cotton balls

✔ other materials with texture

✔ glue stick

Setup

Instructional Sequence

1. Lead a class discussion about the senses: "Who can tell me what sense we used for the first page?" (sight) "What other senses are there?"

2. Explain that students will work on the second page of the book. Read aloud the sentence at the top of the page: "I like the feel of _____ because _____."

3. Brainstorm with students about what they can write for the second page.

4. Explain that after the students write their sentences on half the page, they will create pictures on the other half that represent what they like to touch. They can draw what they like to touch with pastels or crayons and then glue on material that feels similar to the object they've drawn. For example, if a student likes the feel of bunnies, he or she might draw a bunny and glue on a cotton ball for its tail.

Assessment

Throughout this activity, assess student comprehension and effort:

- Do students understand the five senses during class discussion?

- Do students put care and effort into writing and art about what they enjoy touching?

I like the feel of leaves because they are soft and fragile.

Activity 3 *(continued)*

I Like the Feel Of . . .

Variations

- The class could discuss the senses the day before working on the second page of the book. Ask students to bring in materials they like to touch. (Make sure they understand that the materials they bring in will be part of an art project.)

- Older students could also work on multimedia art projects, using materials as well as pastels or colored pencils, but their subject would be more abstract than the sense of touch. For example, they might use materials that represent a concept such as fear, regret, or joy. Instead of sentences, they might write an essay about their artwork: the overall concept of their piece, how the material they chose represents the concept, and how the concept affects their lives (such as specific fears, regrets, or times of joy).

--- **Activity 4** ---

I Like the Taste Of . . .

About This Activity

This fourth activity of the All about Me unit continues student exploration of the senses, this time focusing on the sense of taste and how taste can evoke feelings as well as reflect personality.

Materials

- ✔ third page of book (See page 129.)
- ✔ construction paper (many colors)
- ✔ glue stick

Setup

Instructional Sequence

1. Continue the discussion of the senses you began in the previous activity: "What senses have we used? Which ones are left?" (You could also show student work from the previous activities.)

2. Explain that students will work on the third page of the book. Read aloud the sentence at the top of the page: "The taste of _____ makes me feel_____ because _____."

3. Brainstorm with students about what they can write for the third page.

4. Explain that after the students write their sentences, they will create pictures that represent what they like to taste, using torn construction paper they will glue to the bottom of page 3. (They shouldn't use scissors; they can tear the paper carefully into big and small shapes.) Use an example if needed: If a student likes the taste of ice cream sundaes, for example, he or she could use a white semi-circle for the bowl, brown and pink circles for the ice cream, and a smaller red circle for the cherry.

Assessment

Throughout this activity, assess student comprehension and effort:

- Do students understand how different tastes can evoke different feelings in themselves?

- Do students put thought and effort into writing about and depicting tastes that evoke personal feelings?

Variations

- Students could draw or paint their taste pictures.

- Older students could focus on more complex issues surrounding the sense of taste, such as the use of taste tests in marketing, the scientific processes involved in our sense of taste (such as how taste buds work or the different areas of our tongues that taste sweet, sour, bitter, and so forth), or the meaning of *taste* in the sense of individual preferences and how we judge each other and ourselves by this sense of taste.

Activity 5
I Like the Sound Of . . .

About This Activity

This fifth activity of the All about Me unit enables students to explore the sense of sound, such as how the sounds they like to hear reflect who they are.

Materials

- ✔ fourth page of book (See page 130.)
- ✔ half sheets of white construction paper
- ✔ black markers
- ✔ tissue paper
- ✔ glue and water mixture (one part glue to one part water)
- ✔ paint brushes
- ✔ glue stick

Setup

Instructional Sequence

1. Continue the discussion of senses you began in previous activities: "What senses have we explored? What is left?"

2. Explain that students will work on the fourth page of the book. Read aloud the sentence at the top of the page: "I like the sound of _____ because _____."

3. Brainstorm with students about what they can write for the fourth page.

4. Explain that after the students write their sentences, they will create pictures, using black marker and tissue paper, showing what makes the sounds they like (such as a bird or musical instrument).

5. First they will draw the picture on the white construction paper with a black marker.

6. Then they will cover it with a layer of colored tissue paper (any colors they choose) and paint a light coat of glue-and-water mixture over the top.

7. When the mixture dries, the students will glue the picture onto page 4.

Assessment

Throughout this activity, assess student comprehension and effort:

- ■ Do students understand hearing as a sense?

- ■ Do students put thought and effort into writing about and depicting the sounds they like?

Variations

- For extra credit, students could record sounds they like (or dislike) and present the tapes to the class, narrating each sound (or having the class guess).

- Older students could explore more complex issues surrounding sound, such as noise pollution, the processes involved in hearing (such as how the ear works), how sounds can work together to create a new sound (such as musical instruments), or the effects of sound on mood.

--- **Activity 6** ---

I Like the Smell Of . . .

About This Activity

This sixth activity of the All about Me unit helps students explore how smells connect to memories.

Materials

✔ fifth page of book (See page 131.)
✔ colored chalk
✔ half sheets of black construction paper
✔ glue stick
✔ objects with strong smells (see Setup)

Setup

Bring in objects with strong smells, such as cinnamon, roses, incense, rubber, an onion, or mentholated salve.

Instructional Sequence

1. Continue the discussion of the senses you began in previous activities: "What senses have we explored? What is left?"

2. Lead a discussion about the connection between smell and memory. Pass around objects with strong smells and ask students what these scents remind them of, if anything.

3. Explain that students will work on the fifth page of the book. Read aloud the sentence at the top of the page: "The smell of _____ makes me remember _____ because _____."

4. Brainstorm with students about what they can write for the fifth page.

5. Explain that after the students write their sentences, they will create pictures that represent the smell and what the smell reminds them of, using colored chalk on black construction paper.

6. Students then glue the picture onto page 5.

Assessment

Throughout this activity, assess student comprehension and effort:

■ Do students understand the connection between smells and memories?

■ Do students put thought and effort into choosing a smell and its corresponding memory?

Variations

• Students could bring objects to class that have particular smells and memory associations. Students sit in a circle and take turns passing each object around and describing the memory.

• Older students might try a more complex exploration of smell, such as researching how humans smell, writing a short story or poem that begins with a smell and memory association, or keeping a journal of memories, each entry beginning with a particular smell.

• Students could tell a story while other students listen with eyes closed. The storyteller would bring in different smells to accompany different parts of the story (such as a particular food smell if the story includes food, or the smell of a particular flower if that flower, or flowers in general, appear in the story).

Activity 7

I Hope

About This Activity

This final activity in the All about Me unit helps students explore the idea of hope and express their own hopes through writing and art.

Materials

✔ sixth page of book (See page 132.)

✔ crayons

✔ watercolors (crayon resistant)

✔ glue stick

Setup

Instructional Sequence

1. Remind students what they did with the first five pages of the book (sight, touch, taste, sound, smell). Show a few examples of student work from previous activities, then explain that the sixth page is not about one of the five senses. It is about hope. Explain that thinking about our hopes is another way to discover more about who we are.

2. Explain that students will work on the sixth and final page of the book. Read aloud the sentence at the top of the page: "I hope
   _____."

3. Explain that for this page, the students should think of something they could hope for that would make the world a better place, their classroom a better place, or themselves better people.

4. Brainstorm with students about what they can write for the sixth page. Add your own thoughts if the students need some ideas. Explore the idea of hope: "What does it really mean?" "Why is it important to humans?" Students should think about how they can make their hopes become reality.

5. Explain that after the students write their sentences, they will create pictures that represent what they hope for by outlining with crayon and then brushing the outline with watercolors.

6. When the pictures dry, the students will glue their pictures onto page 6.

Assessment

Throughout this activity, assess student comprehension and effort:

- Do students understand the concept of hope? Can they apply it to their own lives?

- Do students follow directions, choosing a hope that will help better the world, the classroom, or themselves?

- Do students put thought and effort into writing about and depicting their hopes?

Hope flows freely from the hearts of children.

Activity 7 *(continued)*
I Hope

Variations

- Students could write poems instead of sentences: Each line should start with the words "I hope."

- Older students could take this activity a step further and develop a specific plan to make their hopes come true, then put that plan into action (as individuals or in groups). For example, a hope that the world will still have clean air in 20 years may lead students to develop a plan to cut pollution (writing to congress, writing to local businesses, writing editorials for the paper, researching local pollution, and so forth).

Every gift of noble origin
Is breathed upon by Hope's perpetual breath.
—William Wordsworth

Multiple Intelligences

Standards
(See pages 122–23.)

- Reading
- Writing
- Communication
- Art

Guiding Concepts
(See pages viii–x.)

- Meaning making
- Intuitive knowing
- Emotion
- Creativity
- Connections
- Self-reflection

Multiple Intelligences
(See page 124.)

- All

About This Unit

In this unit, students explore the multiple intelligences (MI): how the intelligences are different in different people; how people use them; and how each student has a unique combination of intelligences, some stronger than others. Students will learn about and use the intelligences through the following activities:

1. Ways People Are Smart (1 1/2 hours over two days)

2. Observing Multiple Intelligences (30 minutes)

3. Ways to Tell a Story (20 minutes)

4. Telling a Story with Multiple Intelligence Strengths (3–4 hours, including presentations, plus time over several weeks for students to read stories on their own)

Goals

- Students will learn about and appreciate ways people are smart.

- Students will discover ways they are smart.

- Students will learn from each other and learn to observe and notice other people's approaches to situations and projects.

- Students will use their strongest intelligence to tell a story.

Some children learn best with hands-on activities.

Time

4 activities during 1 week (See specific times in About This Unit.)

Grade Range

1–4

Assessment for This Unit

Keep the following questions in mind throughout the unit. See individual activities for more specific assessment ideas.

- Do students participate in class discussions?

- Do students express thoughts effectively using the multiple intelligences?

- Do students follow directions?

- Do students incorporate the language of multiple intelligences into their vocabularies and begin to notice the intelligences of other people?

- Are students able to discover and articulate what their intelligence strengths and weaknesses are?

Unit Variations

- You could adapt the unit for older students: Assign reading about multiple intelligences; use age-appropriate books and videos (see suggestions on page 138); assign projects that are about and use multiple intelligences to help students develop an in-depth understanding of the intelligences.

- You could expand the unit to include a different activity that focuses on each intelligence. For example, to focus on the musical-rhythmic intelligence, students could create songs to help them remember each intelligence; to focus on naturalist intelligence, students could think about what animals they associate with each intelligence (such as a peacock as visual-spatial, a mockingbird as verbal-linguistic, a school of fish as interpersonal, and so forth).

Activity 1

Ways People Are Smart

About This Activity

This first activity of the Multiple Intelligences unit encourages children to consider the many ways in which people are smart *before* they learn about the multiple intelligences. Then they apply their understanding of multiple intelligences by creating tableaux.

Materials

✔ whiteboard (with pens) or chalkboard (with chalk)

✔ strips of paper (or pieces of tagboard)

✔ tape

Setup

After the first day of this activity, you will need to transfer the first day's ideas to sentence strips for the second day.

Instructional Sequence

1. On the first day of the activity (out of two days), ask students: "What are some ways in which you are smart?"

2. Write student suggestions on the board, guiding the discussion if needed to get it started. At the end of class (or at the end of the day) transfer the student suggestions to the strips of paper (called *sentence strips*) or tagboard in preparation for the second day of the activity.

3. The next day, explain that a famous man, Howard Gardner, wrote a book about ways people are intelligent. He called these ways *multiple intelligences.*

4. Write the intelligences on the board in kid words, leaving space to tape the sentence strips next to or beneath each intelligence. (See Kid Words box on this page.) Explain how Gardner defined each intelligence.

5. Remind students of the brainstorming they did the previous day and explain that they were able to come up with many of the intelligences on their own.

6. Read a sentence strip and ask students what intelligence it should go under. Tape it under the corresponding intelligence written on the board. Repeat for each sentence strip.

7. When you believe that most students understand multiple intelligences, explain that they will break into groups and do *tableaux* (motionless and silent scenes) to depict intelligences for the class. For each tableau, the class will guess which intelligence the group is modeling. (At a later date, groups can show their tableaux to another class that is learning about multiple intelligences.)

8. Assign three students to each group and whisper an intelligence to each group. Groups have 5 to 10 minutes to practice their tableaux; then the class comes together for sharing and guessing.

Kid Words

Logical-mathematical .... Number Smart

Verbal-linguistic .... Word Smart

Bodily-kinesthetic .... Body Smart

Interpersonal .... People Smart

Intrapersonal .... Self Smart

Naturalist .... Nature Smart

Visual-spatial .... Picture Smart

Musical-rhythmic .... Music Smart

Activity 1 *(continued)*

Ways People Are Smart

Assessment

Throughout the activity, assess student comprehension, participation, and effort:

- Do students participate in class discussions?

- Do students understand the idea that people are smart in different ways, and that these different ways can be categorized as multiple intelligences?

- Do students work well in groups?

Variations

- You could write the intelligences on strips of paper and put them in a hat or other container for groups to draw from, instead of telling each group what tableau to perform.

- You could adapt this activity for older students by teaching the actual multiple intelligence terminology (instead of the kid words).

Human nature is not a machine to be built after a model, and set to do exactly the work prescribed for it, but a tree, which requires to grow and develop itself on all sides, according to the tendency of the inward forces which make it a living thing.

—John Stuart Mill

Activity 2

Observing Multiple Intelligences

About This Activity

This second activity of the Multiple Intelligences unit helps students solidify and apply their understanding of the intelligences by observing intelligence in others.

Materials

- ✔ TV and VCR

- ✔ *Rugrats* video (or any video that has characters who demonstrate the multiple intelligences; see suggestions on page 138)

- ✔ Observing Multiple Intelligences sheet (See page 133.)

Setup

- Get VCR and TV ready to show video.

- Make copies of observation sheets.

Instructional Sequence

1. Ask the class: "Who can tell me what the multiple intelligences are?" Discuss briefly until all intelligences are given.

2. Pass out observation sheets and explain that the students are going to watch about 15 minutes of a video and observe the characters.

Students should make notes on the observation sheet about which intelligences they observe the characters using. (You might want to point out a few examples within the first few minutes of the video.)

3. After watching the video, ask students to share their observations and explain why they chose the intelligences they did for the characters.

Assessment

Assess student comprehension:

- Do students demonstrate an understanding of multiple intelligences based on their observations?

- Can students explain their answers (using critical thinking)?

Variations

- Students could observe another classroom or other children at recess and write down what multiple intelligences they see. They should be able to explain their answers.

- You could expand this activity to include additional videos or books, such as the Harry Potter series, in which characters exhibit the intelligences. (See page 138 for more suggestions.)

- Students could observe family members and write down what intelligences they see.

Activity 3
Ways to Tell a Story

About This Activity

In this third activity of the Multiple Intelligences unit, students brainstorm ways to tell a story using all of the intelligences. They create a visual reminder of these ways to use for the next activity.

Materials

✔ poster board

✔ markers

Setup

Children tell stories with pictures.

Instructional Sequence

1. Ask the class, "How do people tell stories?"

2. Write down all of the student suggestions.

3. Encourage them to broaden their ideas. In addition to writing and reading, you might suggest songs, recitation, dance, play, claymation, comic strips, videos, and pictures.

4. Make a poster of all of the ideas for telling a story using different intelligences to use with the next activity.

Assessment

Throughout this activity, assess student participation and comprehension:

▪ Do students participate in the group discussion?

▪ Do student answers demonstrate their knowledge of multiple intelligences?

Variations

- You could combine this activity with the next (Telling a Story Using Multiple Intelligence Strengths), brainstorming ways to tell a story (after students have completed the homework of the next activity) that illuminates their own multiple intelligence strengths and weaknesses.

- Instead of creating a poster as a class, each student could work on his or her own individual poster after the class brainstorms ideas.

--- **Activity 4** ---

Telling a Story Using Multiple Intelligence Strengths

About This Activity

This fourth and final activity of the Multiple Intelligences unit helps students explore their own intelligence strengths and weakness and how they can use their strengths to tell stories.

Materials

✔ My Multiple Intelligences sheet (See page 134.)

✔ books with lessons or characters who have admirable qualities (See suggestions on page 136.)

✔ poster of ways to tell a story (from previous activity)

Setup

A week before this activity, send home the homework so it will be turned in before this activity. Each student should get three Multiple Intelligences sheets: one for illustrating the student's intelligences and the others for illustrating two family members' intelligences. Demonstrate for the class how to color in the MI circle based on your strengths and weaknesses before you send the work home.

Instructional Sequence

1. Choose one student's homework and ask if you can show it to the rest of the class.

2. Discuss the multiple intelligence circle with the class (noting which strength this particular student believes she or he has).

3. Point out the poster that lists ways to tell a story and ask which way the student might choose to tell a story based on his or her intelligence strengths. (For example, a word-smart student might write or tell a story; a body-smart student might perform a dance to tell the story; a picture-smart student might choose to create a comic strip to the tell the story.)

4. Repeat the process with another student's homework until students understand the connection between individual strengths and how one can use those strengths to tell a story.

5. Introduce stories that have admirable characters or lessons (fictional or real) and explain that students should think about which story they would like to read, which plot or characters interest them.

6. Tell students that after they read their chosen stories, they will each choose which way they would like to tell the story to an audience.

7. During the next several weeks, students will read their stories and work on their storytelling ideas. They will prepare for a storytelling event before an audience.

8. For the event, students will tell their stories in their chosen ways, also presenting in some fashion what they learned from the stories (lessons, qualities of people, and so forth). Again, they can present in any way that demonstrates an intelligence: talking, creating a poster, singing, dancing, and so on.

Assessment

Throughout the activity, assess student effort and comprehension:

- Do students demonstrate their understanding of multiple intelligences by choosing a way to tell their stories that uses their own strengths?

- Do students comprehend the stories they have chosen as demonstrated by their retellings of the stories and the lessons they learned?

- Do students present their ideas clearly to others?

Activity 4 *(continued)*

Telling a Story Using Multiple Intelligence Strengths

Variations

- Instead of choosing a strength, students could tell a story to work on a weak area.

- Students could write their own stories to tell, or ask parents and grandparents for family stories.

- You could tie this into a storytelling unit during which an artist-in-residence comes to tell stories from her or his culture. Children will then retell the stories in their own ways.

My Culture

Standards
(See pages 122–23.)

- Writing
- Communication
- Science
- Social Studies
- Art

Guiding Concepts
(See pages viii–x.)

- Meaning making
- Religion (objective study)
- Creativity
- Connections
- Self-reflection

Multiple Intelligences
(See page 124.)

- Verbal-linguistic
- Visual-spatial
- Intrapersonal
- Interpersonal
- Naturalist

About This Unit

In this unit, students explore the concept of culture by examining their own lives and those of their families through the following activities:

1. My Culture Map (1 hour)
2. Autobiography (1–2 hours)
3. Defining Family (45 minutes)
4. Family Tree and Interview (1 hour)
5. Culture Poster (1–2 hours)

Goals

- Students will define *family* and learn more about their own families, including people who are special to them but aren't blood relatives.

- Students will learn more about their identities as members of their families and of a larger culture.

- Students will make connections with their elders and learn where some of their family and cultural beliefs and traditions originated.

Time

Approximately 5–9 hours over 3 weeks (See time frames for each activity above.)

Grade Range

3–8

Family traditions and history help weave the rich tapestry of culture.

Assessment for This Unit

Keep the following questions in mind throughout the unit. See individual activities for more specific assessment ideas.

- Do students complete all assignments?
- Do students participate in class discussions?
- Do students use critical-thinking skills to examine their own lives and the lives of their families?
- Do students represent their cultures with care and thought?
- Do students respect other students' cultural representations and discussion?

Unit Variations

- You could add a research project to the unit: Students could research and report on the countries their families are from, the religion they practice (if any), or the genealogy of their families.

- Students could create a family book, with a page for each family member that includes photos and biographical information.

- You could expand the unit to have students study the culture of other students. Pair up students of different backgrounds and adapt the activities in this unit so that each student creates a cultural poster for his or her partner.

No one is a light unto himself, not even the sun.
—Antonio Porchia

Activity 1
My Culture Map

About This Activity

This first activity of the My Culture unit will help students visualize the influences that shape who they are.

Materials

✔ 1 piece of poster board (2 x 2 feet)

✔ paper

✔ colored pens or pencils

Setup

Think about the elements of your own culture map: What and who in your life shaped who you are today? Your map might include things like gender, relationships (mother or father, sister or brother, daughter or son, and so forth), occupation, era you grew up in, religion, ethnic background, and so forth.

Instructional Sequence

1. Draw your culture map on the poster board: Write down one influence on your life and draw a circle around it. The size of the circle represents the level of influence. Write down another influence and draw a circle around it. Some circles will overlap others (for example,

your role as "daughter" may overlap "wife" because you formed your ideas of "wife" from your parents' model).

2. Ask students to brainstorm as a class what might go on their culture maps. When necessary, suggest ideas to help them think in new directions, such as those mentioned in Setup above as well as holidays, foods, traditional family trips or vacations, and family sayings. List ideas on the board.

3. Ask students to get out a piece of paper and brainstorm for their own culture maps.

4. After they have brainstormed, ask students to create their culture maps.

Assessment

Keep the following questions in mind throughout this activity:

▪ Do students participate in class discussion?

▪ Do students respect other students' suggestions?

▪ Do students understand and represent the connections among influences in their lives?

Variations

- Culture maps could be more complex, including different shapes and colors as well as different sizes to represent types of influences. For example, students could use the same color to indicate similar influences (such as blue circles around friends' names) and shapes to represent the type of influence (such as a guitar outline around a musical influence).

- Culture maps could include pictures (drawn or cut out and pasted) to represent influences instead of, or in addition to, words.

- Students could work on culture maps in pairs, enabling them to talk about their cultures and influences and help each other come up with more connections and ideas through discussion.

- Students could work in pairs to create culture maps for each other by interviewing each other about family, friends, customs, religion, places they've lived, and other influences.

Activity 2
Autobiography

About This Activity

In this second activity in the My Culture unit, students use their culture maps (from the previous activity) as a basis for writing their autobiographies.

My brother is an important part of my family.

Materials

✔ culture maps (from Culture Map activity)

✔ paper

✔ pencils or pens

✔ computer (optional)

Setup

Choose one or two aspects of your culture map and write a one-page autobiography that expands on these influences.

Instructional Sequence

1. Display your culture map and read your autobiography to the class.

2. Ask students if they could tell which part of your culture map you wrote about in your autobiography. Explain if they don't make the connections.

3. Ask students to choose part of their culture maps to expand on and begin rough drafts of their autobiographies (required length is dependent on age of students).

4. Students should edit their rough drafts and type them up on the computer (if one is available).

Assessment

Consider the following questions:

- Do students use the writing process (prewriting, drafting, revising, editing, publishing) and attempt to develop the writing traits (ideas, organization, voice, word choice, sentence fluency, conventions, presentation)?

- Do student papers reflect their culture maps?

Variations

- Each student could write a biography of another student based on the other student's culture map.

- Students could write their autobiographies in installments, throughout a quarter, semester, or year. Each installment (or chapter) would illuminate a different area of the culture map. Allow students to add to their culture maps, too, as the year progresses and they get to know themselves better.

Activity 3

Defining Families

About This Activity

In this third activity in the My Culture unit, students discuss and explore the meaning and definition of *family*.

Materials

✔ paper

✔ pencils or pens

Setup

Bring in a photograph of your family, as well as a picture of someone who isn't a relative but is special to you—someone you consider family.

Instructional Sequence

1. Show your first family photo and introduce the family members to your class: "This is my family. This is my father, brother, daughter, . . ."

2. Start a discussion about the definition of family. Ask students to share their ideas. (Expect answers like mom, dad, grandparents, stepfamily, adopted families, maybe two-mom or two-dad families.)

3. Show your other photo and explain that this person is special to you and you consider this person your family also.

4. Continue discussing the definition of family as a class.

5. Explain to students that they will be making a poster that represents their culture, which will probably include their families. Ask them to start thinking about what they want to include on their posters (photographs, stories, mementos, and so forth).

6. Explain to students that they will interview their families to find out about family traditions, beliefs, and stories. Ask them to brainstorm some interview questions.

7. Have a whole class discussion to share ideas that students came up with for interview questions and items to include on their posters. Suggest any ideas you think are missing.

Assessment

Throughout this activity, assess student participation and comprehension:

- Do students participate in and respect each other during class discussion?

- Do students show an understanding of the flexible nature of families?

Variations

- Students could bring in photo-graphs of family and people who are special to them or to their families before having the discussion about families.

- Older students could write an essay about the meaning and definition of family before you discuss families as a class. Then ask them to write a follow-up essay after the class discussion.

Activity 4

Family Tree and Interview

About This Activity

In this fourth activity in the My Culture unit, students connect with family members to create family trees and learn about family history, traditions, and stories.

Materials

✔ paper

✔ pens or pencils

Setup

Instructional Sequence

1. Ask students if they know what a family tree is.

2. Guide a brief discussion about family trees. Remind students of the definitions of family they brainstormed during the previous activity. In their family trees, they can include those special people in their lives who aren't related by blood, marriage, or adoption.

3. Draw the beginning of your family tree on the board to show how family trees are organized. Ask students to fill in a few (for example, "If my grandmother's mom's name was Anne, where would I put that on my family tree?").

4. Pass out paper and pens or pencils and ask students to spend about 15 to 20 minutes creating their family trees, filling in what they can on their own.

5. Tell students that they will work with their families to fill in as much as they can for homework.

   In addition, for homework, students will interview family members (using interview questions they developed during the previous activity) and begin rough drafts of short stories and poems from the information they gather.

6. Students will edit stories and poems and then make final copies of those and the family trees to add to their culture posters.

Assessment

During and after the activity, assess student comprehension and effort:

- Do students understand how to apply the concept and structure of family trees to their own families?

- Do students complete all assignments?

- Do students use the writing process (prewriting, drafting, revising, editing, publishing) and develop the writing traits (ideas, organization, voice, word choice, sentence fluency, conventions, presentation) in their stories or poems?

Variations

- For younger students, you might divide the family tree and family interview into two activities, so they can focus on one at a time.

- The family tree could be an art project as well: Provide art supplies (such as colored pencils, crayons, or pastels) for students to use in decorating their trees. Note: They don't *have* to stick with the image of a tree. Students could draw a skyscraper or a mountain or anything that will allow for the horizontal and vertical structure of the family tree names.

- Older students could work on a more complex genealogy assignment: Research ancestry as far back as possible and create a map that shows family origin and movement, as well as the current location of various family members.

Activity 5

Culture Poster

About This Activity

This fifth and final activity in the My Culture unit is a culmination of all the activities in this unit: a poster that includes photographs with explanations, family trees, culture maps, autobiographies, stories or poems, and other items that depict each student's unique culture.

Materials

- ✔ large pieces of cardboard for poster backing
- ✔ glue
- ✔ markers
- ✔ tape
- ✔ miscellaneous art supplies (anything you have available)

Setup

Students should bring in all of the photographs and other personal materials they want to add to their posters, in addition to the final products of the previous activities in this unit.

Instructional Sequence

1. Explain what students need to include on their posters: photographs and other personal items with explanations; family tree; culture map; autobiography; and story or poem based on the family interview. They should attach all materials to the cardboard backing.

2. Give students the opportunity to work on their posters.

3. Students then present their finished posters to the class and display them in the hall for the school to see.

Assessment

During and after this activity, assess student comprehension and effort:

- Do students include all required materials on their posters?

- Are students respectful to each other as they work on their posters (sharing supplies, commenting on others' work, and so forth)?

Variations

- Students could have a family night for their families to listen to presentations about the culture posters.

- Students could create a class culture poster, instead of individual posters. Cover a wall with paper for students to decorate and post family trees, photographs, and other items.

Every man is more than just himself; he also represents the unique, the very special and always significant and remarkable point at which the world's phenomena intersect, only once in this way and never again.

—Herman Hesse

More Thematic Unit Ideas

- **Festivals of Light:** Students could join in the fun of festivals from around the world that focus on light during the darkest part of the year—winter. They learn about different cultures' celebrations and traditions through reading, writing, art, and sharing. This unit is taught during the winter holidays (the month of December). Festivals of Light can include Loi Krathong, Diwali, Santa Lucia's Day, Hanukkah, Las Posadas, A Philippine Christmas, Kwanzaa, and so forth. You can add different celebrations that your students celebrate.

  Students learn the background of each festival and enjoy activities, recipes, and songs. They make pieces that bring light to each culture's celebration from clay, candles, paper, and other materials: for example, dipa (Diwali), krathong (Loi Krathong), menorah (Hanukkah), farolito (Las Posadas), kinara (Kwanzaa), and a Christmas tree ornament (Christmas). The class holds a culminating Festival of Light before winter break. Each student can choose one of the art projects to light during the festival (optional), and students or parents can make traditional festival foods, sing songs, and share family traditions. For more information about this unit idea, see *Festivals of Light: A Hands-on Activity Book,* by Margaret Elmer, Charlotte Beall, and Sarah Robertson (see page 140 for more details). Other resources are listed on page 140, under Celebrations and Traditions.

- **About My State:** Students can focus on the religious and cultural history and present makeup of the state in addition to studying the state's geography, political systems and people, notable cities, and so forth. Activities might include group work to present skits about historical events, to teach each other facts, to learn traditional dances or songs of various cultural groups in the state, and to create travel brochures or almanacs about the state. Individual work might include essays on state events, drawings of inventions created in the state, portraits of notable figures, journal entries from the perspective of the state's most creative people, and multimedia guidebooks that describe and depict the state's flora and fauna.

- **Life of Animals:** Activities might focus on the classifications of animals, animal life cycles, animal habitats, and the interconnectedness of various animals, covering a range of animal species. Students could create ecosystem murals, animal yearbooks (with pictures of various animals accompanied by each animal's achievements, motto, future goals, "most likely to . . ." designation, and so forth), drawings of and stories about new species the students create, plays about animal interaction, journal entries from the perspective of an animal, songs about an animal (or a class orchestra of different animal sounds), poems about the lessons humans can learn from a particular animal, and so forth.

- **Vacation:** As a class, students could choose one place they would most like to visit in the world, outside of the United States. Activities would center on planning an imaginary vacation to this place: learn the basics of the language; explore climate and weather to determine the best time of year to go; solve a word problem that involves scheduling the class trip despite many different student schedule conflicts; create a packing list; read stories about the country; research the cultural, religious, and political history of the region; write to pen pals; map out the trip; and so forth.

- **Religions of the World:** This unit would involve objective study of religions, including history; traditions; creation stories; guiding principles; prominent figures; important texts, art, and music; and so forth. Activities might include creating a world calendar with holidays, traditions, and other special dates for every religion marked; the Creation Stories activity on page 2; imaginary discussions between prominent religious figures; discussion of the purposes and meaning of religion; essays that explore similarities among religions; religion time lines; dioramas of religious events (from various religions); stories or poetry about the connections between religions and nature; collages of religious art (from various religions); and so forth.

Add your own ideas:

Chapter 8
Yearlong Themes

Character

About This Theme

This yearlong theme involves four units to explore four aspects of character:

1. Respect

2. Courage

3. Generosity

4. Pride

Each unit can span a quarter (as in this book) or one to two weeks. You can tailor the units to meet your curriculum needs and student ages using activity and project ideas from the following pages.

Goals

- Students will define respect, generosity, courage, and pride.

- Students will incorporate actions of respect, generosity, courage, and pride into classroom activities throughout the year and into their daily lives.

- Students will create a classroom community based on their learning about and collective actions to develop respect, generosity, courage, and pride.

Grade Range

K–8

Resources

The materials and resources you need will depend on the activities and projects you choose from the following pages. See *Character Education*, by Heidel & Lyman-Mersereau (1999), and the books listed on page 142 for additional ideas.

Assessment for This Theme

Keep the following questions in mind as your students explore character throughout the year. See individual units, on the following pages, for assessment ideas specific to each unit.

- Do students participate in class discussions?

- Do students follow directions?

- Do students complete all assignments?

- Do students apply learning about character to other classroom activities?

- Do students incorporate these aspects of character into their daily lives?

Variations

- You could add your own activity and project ideas to support the character focus of each quarter.

- You could alter the order of the units (for example, start with pride the first quarter), or create new units based on other aspects of character, such as honesty or responsibility.

- You might discuss definitions and components of character with your students, then structure units based on your and your students' ideas.

Unit 1
Respect

Activities and Projects

- Preassess understanding by asking your students, "What is respect?" Discuss as a class or have students fast-write answers to the question (20 minutes).

- Ask students why respect is important and how they can show respect in the classroom. Create a class list of respectful behavior (30 minutes).

- Have students practice respecting others' work with the Rotating Art activity, on page 34 (1 hour).

- Read stories throughout the quarter about respect, such as *The Doll Lady,* by Collins and Kuusisto, or *I Like Me!,* by Carlson. (See additional suggestions on page 136.) Discuss each story, its lessons, and how students can apply what they have learned to their own lives (25 minutes of discussion per story, plus time for teacher or students to read each story, depending on its complexity and the students' reading level).

- Have students choose people they respect from history, read a book about them, write a report, and present to the class (10 minutes' presentation time per student, plus 1 hour for teacher to present and explain lesson, and time for students to read story and work on reports; some time can be spent as homework).

- Discuss the definition of the Golden Rule (basically, treat others as you want to be treated). Research how this rule is phrased in the writings of various cultures and religions (30 minutes to 2 hours, depending on depth of research).

- Have students make posters to illustrate the Golden Rule in practice around the world (1 hour).

- Have students keep a journal about their experiences, inside and outside the classroom, with respect and the Golden Rule throughout the quarter (20 minutes per week).

- Ask parents and guardians to write letters about how their children are respectful outside of school (no class time).

- Brainstorm with the class a list of ways they can show respect for themselves. For example, taking care of their bodies, following their consciences, being honest, being themselves, and so forth (20 minutes).

- Ask your students to write personal lists of ways they can respect themselves every day (20 minutes).

- Have students research ways to respect the Earth (for example, recycle, conserve water and electricity, eat organic foods, compost, don't use chemicals, be kind to other living things, and so forth). Students (in groups or individually) then create posters from their research to display in the hall or classroom (4 hours).

- Have students write a poem, song, story, or essay about respect. Topics might include respect for the Earth, respect for their peers, respect for differences, self-respect, the Golden Rule in their daily lives, or the Golden Rule as practiced (or not practiced) in their communities and around the world (10 minutes class time to discuss the assignment).

- Have a Respect Party (2 hours):
  - Display Golden Rule posters, respect the Earth posters, and art projects.
  - Ask parents and guardians to come to the party and read the letters they wrote about their children.

—— **Unit 1** *(continued)* ——

Respect

- Have snacks and watch a video about respect, such as *Shrek* (self-respect), *Fern Gully* (respect for nature), or *Rudy* (earning respect).

Assessment

The following questions are for evaluation of the various activities and projects listed above. Assessment depends on which activities and projects you choose.

- Do students use the writing process (pre-writing, drafting, revising, editing, publishing) to complete papers?

- Do students show attention to the writing traits (ideas, organization, voice, word choice, sentence fluency, conventions, presentation) in their papers?

- Do students respect each other during group work?

- Do students respect you and other students during whole group activities, including discussions?

- Do students show comprehension skills during discussions of respect stories?

- Do students respect you and each other throughout the school year, even when not working on this unit?

Unit 2
Generosity

Activities and Projects

- Preassess understanding: Have students in small groups brainstorm definitions and examples of generosity on big pieces of paper, then share with the class (20 minutes).

- Choose a charity to help (can be chosen by teacher or students as age appropriate), such as hurricane or earthquake relief, a food bank, make-a-wish foundation, or after-school activities for inner-city kids. As a class, decide how to help: Volunteering? Collecting food? Raising money? (30 minutes of class time) (See Giving a Million activity, page 24.)

- Read stories to students (or have students read independently) that revolve around generosity, such as books about Thanksgiving, Hanukkah, Christmas, Chinese New Year, and other winter celebrations (25 minutes each). (See suggested titles on pages 136–37.)

- Have students make presents for homeless children, such as beaded friendship bracelets, cookies, cards, or painted tiles (1 hour).

- Have the class create and decorate a donation box and encourage students to donate old toys to underprivileged kids by putting them in the donation box (30 minutes of class time).

- Have students make friendship bracelets for reading buddies (30 minutes). (See page 5 for Buddy Reading activity.)

- Assign generosity poems: Students talk to friends, family, or teachers about generous acts and write poems about these acts (1–2 hours, unless homework).

- Have students write about how they are generous during the holidays and how they can continue to be generous throughout the year (2 hours, unless homework).

- Have students search newspapers and magazines for stories about generous people and acts. They can create a book of the articles, write responses to the stories, create a mural or dioramas depicting the acts, or write a news story about themselves or another person in the class being generous (3 hours).

- Have students write about the generosity of family members or friends and what it meant to them (1 hour).

- Have students write the word "generosity" on a piece of drawing paper and then draw it (that is, express or represent a feeling or value in a drawing). They could depict a generous act or be more abstract (30 minutes).

- Have students create a recipe for cooking up generosity. (For example: one kind person, two helping hands, and so forth.) (30 minutes)

Assessment

The following questions are for evaluation of the various activities and projects listed above. Assessment depends on which activities and projects you choose.

- Do students participate in class-organized charity events?

- Do students demonstrate an understanding of generosity?

- Do students show comprehension skills during discussions of generosity stories?

- Do students show generosity throughout the school year?

- Do students use the writing process (prewriting, drafting, revising, editing, publishing) and develop the writing traits (ideas, organization, voice, word choice, sentence fluency, conventions, presentation)?

Unit 3

Courage

Activities and Projects

- Preassess understanding: Have students pair up or get into small groups and take turns telling about a time when they were courageous or when someone they know was (30 minutes).

- Have students read books about courage (individually), such as Peet's *Cowardly Clyde,* Millman's *Secret of the Peaceful Warrior,* Lindquist's *Summer Soldiers,* or other titles suggested on pages 136–37, and do book reports to present to the class (reading time, plus 3 hours).

- Watch a video about courage (such as *A Bug's Life* or *Rudy*) and discuss as a class (3 hours).

- Have students write about something they are afraid to do (2 hours). From student pieces, create a list of activities that would require courage from students (such as public speaking, eating lunch with older students, riding a Ferris wheel, feeding a horse, and so forth). Throughout the quarter, set up activities and field trips that give students the opportunity to face their fears. Have students share how they felt afterward (1 hour for writing piece; 30 minutes to 4 hours for activities, depending on activities).

- Have students interview teachers and other students about courageous acts during the week and create a weekly newsletter (4 hours per week).

- Have students research someone from the present or past who they believe is courageous. Students collect articles, photos, quotations, and so forth about their choice and create a collage poster to display in the hall. Students could include a writing piece about why they feel the person is courageous. (Examples of courageous people: Harriet Tubman, Martin Luther King, Jackie Robinson, Alan Shepard, Michael J. Fox, and so forth).

- I Would Be Good activity (see page 32).

Assessment

The following questions are for evaluation of the various activities and projects listed above. Assessment depends on which activities and projects you choose.

- Do students use the writing process (prewriting, drafting, revising, editing, publishing) and develop the writing traits (ideas, organization, voice, word choice, sentence fluency, conventions, presentation) in their writing projects?

- Do students demonstrate comprehension skills in class discussion, book-report presentations, and writing?

- Are students able to be courageous on the field trip? (Note: Being able to say "I really don't want to do it" could be considered courage if it is opposite of what the other students are doing.)

Unit 4
Pride

Activities and Projects

- Preassess understanding by asking your students, "What is pride?" Discuss as a class. Discussion should include the concept of "good" pride versus "bad" pride, such as pride that prevents someone from admitting he or she is wrong (20 minutes).

- Read stories about pride, such as *The Big Brag,* by Dr. Seuss, *My Grandma's the Mayor,* by Pellegrino and Lund, or *Some Kind of Pride,* by Testa (30 minutes per session).

- Have students write about a time when they were proud of something they did (1–2 hours).

- Ask parents and guardians to write about a time when they were proud of their children (no class time).

- Make a class poster: "I'm proud to be in this class because . . ." Everyone contributes words and art (1 hour).

- Listen to songs about pride, such as local school fight songs, "God Bless the U.S.A.," by Lee Greenwood, "I Believe I Can Fly," by R. Kelly, or "Pride (In the Name of Love)," by U2, and then write a class song (2 hours).

- Have a Pride Party (2 hours):
  - Display the class poster.
  - Invite parents and guardians to read their letters.
  - Have students share something they are proud of from the last three quarters (such as showing respect, generosity, or courage).
  - Perform the class song.
  - Watch a video about pride (such as *Angels in the Outfield*) while enjoying snacks.

- Each week, focus on one student as the class star. The student can bring in pictures of him or herself, as well as family and friends. Other students can write sentences about what they like about the class star, especially actions and characteristics the student can be proud of.

As the star of the week, a student shares what he is proud of with his classmates.

— **Unit 4** *(continued)* —

Pride

Assessment

The following questions are for evaluation of the various activities and projects listed above. Assessment depends on which activities and projects you choose.

- Do students use the writing process (prewriting, drafting, revising, editing, publishing) to complete papers?

- Do students show attention to the writing traits (ideas, organization, voice, word choice, sentence fluency, conventions, presentation) in their papers?

- Do students demonstrate an understanding of pride?

- Do students participate in and respect each other during class discussions and group work?

> *Character cannot be developed in ease and quiet. Only through experience of trial and suffering can the soul be strengthened, vision cleared, ambition inspired and success achieved.*
>
> —Helen Keller

Clan Animal _____

Standards
(See pages 122–23.)
- All

Guiding Concepts
(See pages viii–x.)
- All

Multiple Intelligences
(See page 124.)
- All

About This Theme

This yearlong theme revolves around one extended unit: clan animal. Students will learn about clans and then choose an animal to represent their class clan. The unit involves in-depth study of the clan animal throughout the year.

Goals

- Students will build a class community by feeling part of a clan.
- Students will study an animal of their choice and the lessons people can learn from this animal.

Grade Range

K–8

Resources

For this theme, you'll need books on clans (see suggestions on page 137) and the clan animal the class chooses, both fiction and nonfiction. After the class chooses an animal, you'll need posters and pictures of that animal to put up around the classroom.

Assessment for This Theme

Keep the following questions in mind as your students explore clans and their clan animal throughout the year. See the individual unit, on page 118, for assessment ideas specific to that unit.

- Do students participate in class discussions and group work?
- Do students follow directions?
- Do students complete all assignments?
- Do students feel part of the class community?

She humbly seeks to learn a lesson from ants, bees, spiders, beavers, and badgers. She studies the family life of the birds, so exquisite in its emotional intensity and its patient devotion.

—Ohiyesa

Variations

- You could expand the unit to create a clan out of an entire grade level or several classes. Alternatively, small groups of students could create clans (and choose different clan animals).

- You could create subgroups in your class based on your clan animal (for example, if your clan animal is an otter, you might have sea otters and river otters, so that sea otters go to the library while river otters stay in class, and then switch).

- You could expand the unit to include study of community and culture as parallels of clans. Incorporate relevant activities from chapters 5, 6, and 7.

- The entire school could participate in the theme: Each class chooses a clan animal in kindergarten or first grade, then keeps that clan animal as a way to promote class unity until the class moves on to middle school. Alternatively, each teacher could choose a clan animal and use it for new incoming students each year (collecting new items and activities about that animal over the years).

Students create a class mural of their clan animal

Unit 1
Class Clan Animal

Activities and Projects

- Read stories (such as those suggested on page 137) that include clans—Native American, Scottish, or other (30 minutes per story).

- Invite a guest speaker, such as a representative of a local Native American tribe—check with your local Native American cultural center (1 hour).

- Choose a clan animal:

  1. Discuss with the class how belonging to a clan is special, how a clan is an extended family. Explain that your class could be considered a clan.

  2. Ask for ideas on an animal to name the class clan after (or choose it yourself). A local animal or one that you can see in a zoo or aquarium will work best for this unit.

  3. Narrow the list to two or three animals (by voting as a class) and read some books about those animals to the class during the next several days (30 minutes per story).

  4. Have students vote on the animal they want, keeping in mind the qualities that the animal has (30 minutes).

- Visit the zoo, aquarium, or a park to observe the animal. Students should take notes in a journal. Discuss lessons that the class can learn from the animal (half day).

- Read stories about the animal periodically (30 minutes each).

- Have students write their own stories about the clan animal. Stories can include facts about the animal as well as lessons (3 hours).

- Assign a research project on the animal, including a final report (8 hours).

- Make a button blanket of the animal. A button blanket is a Northwest Coast Native American blanket (see *The Button Blanket: A Northwest Coast Indian Art Activity Book,* by McNutt). They are typically black on red and use particular shapes and the concept of positive and negative space to create pictures of animals. Buttons are used for borders and decorations. Button blankets can be made out of material or paper and can then be displayed in the classroom or other place in the school (2 hours).

- Have students cut out pictures from magazines or draw pictures of the animal to hang around the classroom (1 hour).

- Have students write and act in a play about the animal (for another class or the entire school). The plan can incorporate lessons learned from the animal (8 hours).

- Create a clan song as a class (1 hour).

- Have students write a poem about what qualities they believe they share with the animal and what qualities they would like to adopt for themselves (for example, otters are playful, active, and curious) (1 hour).

Assessment

Throughout the unit and the year, keep the following questions in mind:

- Do students demonstrate an understanding of the voting process?

- Do students use the writing process (prewriting, drafting, revising, editing, publishing) and develop the writing traits (ideas, organization, voice, word choice, sentence fluency, conventions, presentation) in written work?

- Do students use observation and note-taking skills?

- Do students use critical-thinking skills to figure out what lessons they can learn?

More Yearlong Theme Ideas

- **Heroes:** Throughout the year, students could examine heroes connected to what they are studying, such as heroes of a certain time period or heroes in a certain field. You might prepare lists of names to get kids started and to encourage students to choose heroes from a variety of backgrounds. Units might include heroes of the twentieth century, nineteenth century, eighteenth century, and so forth; heroes in fiction; heroes in science; heroes in government; spiritual heroes; underdog heroes; heroes from students' lives; or heroes of Africa, Asia, South America, and so forth. Activities might include dramatic recreations of events featuring the hero; essays or discussion about what makes the hero a hero; hero murals or comic strips; "A day in the life" essays; biographical sketches of the hero; picture books featuring the hero; research into local heroes; how-to manuals for becoming a hero; songs describing the hero's exploits; and so forth.

- **The Ocean:** Units might include ocean life, history of the ocean, physical composition of the ocean, oceans around the world, and so forth. Activities might include research reports on the pollution and its effects on the ocean; diagrams or murals that demonstrate ocean cycles; writing and art depicting traditions, customs, and legends surrounding the ocean from different cultures; classified ads that describe ocean animals and plants without naming them (for example, "wanted for part-time employment: thin swimming creature with electric personality" for an eel); creating an aquarium version of the ocean; building a model of an underwater city; listening to ocean sounds while writing in journals; and so forth.

- **War and Peace:** Units might include American wars, world wars, wars of the twentieth (or other) century, and world peace. Activities would study war and peace from a historical perspective but also from a philosophical perspective, with a balance between war and peace topics. Students could create and act out interviews with famous peacemakers and activists for peace; write an essay about the reasons behind a particular war; study art produced during or in reaction to war and create similar art pieces; write journal entries about what peace means to them personally; hold a debate among countries involved in a war; interview people who lived through a particular war for a class book of wartime memories; study society, culture, and religion during war versus during peace and create murals depicting major elements; write about common themes in the urban legends that appear during wartime; listen to songs about peace; write about a world without war; and so forth.

Add your own ideas:

Standards and
Multiple Intelligences

Learning Standards _____

Many states have developed academic learning requirements based on the Goals 2000: Educate America Act recommendations. The activities in this guide were developed with the following general academic learning standards in mind.

Reading

Students understand and use several strategies to read, such as word recognition and meaning comprehension, using pictures, sounding out words, and using context. Students use critical-thinking skills to analyze information, comprehend ideas, and evaluate their own progress. Students also use reading for a variety of purposes, such as to obtain new information, to perform a task, or for enjoyment.

Writing

Students write clearly and effectively for different purposes—such as communication with others, self-reflection, and transfer of information—and different audiences, such as friends, coworkers, and the general public. Students understand the writing process (prewriting, drafting, revising, editing, publishing) and evaluate their own work.

The Writing Traits

The following traits serve as guidelines for students to use in creating effective written pieces. (There were originally six traits, but the Northwest Regional Educational Laboratory recently added "Presentation" as a seventh trait. For more details about these traits, see "Scoring 6+1 Trait™ Writing" on the Northwest Regional Educational Laboratory website at www.nwrel.org/assessment/definitions.asp?d=1. See also "Six Traits Writing Assessment" at http://6traits.cyberspaces.net/)

- **Ideas:** The topic makes sense and is interesting and well researched. The written work includes relevant details that keep the readers engaged.

- **Organization:** The written work has a meaningful beginning, a logical progression of events, and a sense of resolution at the end. The work is easy to follow, with sentences that flow well together.

- **Voice:** The personal tone and flavor of the author comes through consistently. The author's passion is apparent in the writing.

- **Word choice:** The author uses rich, colorful words and strong descriptions that expand ideas and help the readers create pictures in their minds. The author takes care to choose the most precise words for the context.

- **Sentence fluency:** The author takes care to vary sentence length and structure and pays attention to the rhythm and flow of sentences so that the work is pleasing to the ear when read aloud.

- **Conventions:** The work is mechanically correct, including effective and correct grammar, punctuation, paragraphing, capitalization, and so forth.

- **Presentation:** The work is presented in a way that is clear, visually appealing, and appropriate to the subject and audience.

Adapted from *Essential Academic Learning Requirements Technical Manual,* published and copyrighted by the Washington State Commission on Student Learning, August 25, 1998. Reprinted with permission of the Superintendent of Public Instruction, State of Washington. A complete listing can be viewed at www.k12.wa.us.

The Writing Process

The following steps are all essential to creating an effective written work, regardless of the work's subject, audience, or purpose.

- **Prewriting:** Brainstorm ideas and topics. Choose a topic. Organize thoughts.

- **Drafting:** Write a rough draft. At this stage, letting the words flow from the mind to the page is more important than correct spelling, punctuation, and so forth.

- **Revising:** Expand on or trim ideas in the rough draft. Add more description as necessary. Clarify ideas.

- **Editing:** Correct spelling, punctuation, grammar, and other mechanical errors. Having another person read through the work is very helpful at this stage.

- **Publishing:** Write a final draft. This may involve just rewriting to include all the corrections and additions from previous stages, or it may involve typing up the work and binding it (with staples or string) or displaying it in some fashion.

Communication

Students communicate to gain understanding by listening, observing, and asking questions. Students use a variety of communication skills, such as speaking, writing (including e-mail), and body language, to work with others and to convey ideas clearly and effectively. Students also evaluate their own progress.

Math

Students understand all the math concepts (number sense, measurement, geometric sense, probability and statistics, and algebraic sense), use critical-thinking skills to solve problems, and communicate mathematical knowledge clearly and effectively.

Science

Students understand and apply scientific concepts (identifying, categorizing, describing substances, and understanding interconnections within systems) and use scientific inquiry to solve problems.

Social Studies

- History: Students understand U.S. and world history (major ideas, eras, themes, developments, turning points, chronology, and cause-and-effect relationships), analyze historical information, and reflect on findings.

- Geography: Students use tools (maps, charts, and so forth) to understand the arrangement of people, places, resources, and environments on the Earth, and to analyze the interaction between people, the environment, and culture.

- Civics: Students understand the principles of U.S. democracy including documents such as the Declaration of Independence and the Constitution; the purpose for governments, laws, and international relationships; and the rights and responsibilities of citizenship.

- Economics: Students understand basic economic concepts and their effects on individuals, groups, and society.

Art

Students understand and use art concepts, such as shading, perspective, and use of color and space, and art forms—including visual arts, music, drama, and dance—to communicate ideas and express their creativity. Students also recognize the connection between art and other subject areas.

Health and Fitness

Students understand and analyze the skills necessary to maintain a healthy life, including physical activity, nutrition, safety, and awareness of environmental factors. Students also acquire skills to develop a personal health plan.

Adapted from *Essential Academic Learning Requirements Technical Manual,* published and copyrighted by the Washington State Commission on Student Learning, August 25, 1998. Reprinted with permission of the Superintendent of Public Instruction, State of Washington. A complete listing can be viewed at www.k12.wa.us.

Multiple Intelligences

For many years, educators assessed children solely by their competence in reading, writing, and mathematics. Howard Gardner believed that there were at least six other ways to be intelligent besides reading and writing (which he called *verbal-linguistic intelligence*) and mathematics (or *logical-mathematical intelligence*). He has written several books detailing his theory of different intelligences, such as *Frames of Mind: The Theory of Multiple Intelligences* (1983) and *Intelligence Reframed: Multiple Intelligences for the 21st Century* (1999), in which he addresses the possibility of spiritual intelligence, among others. As educators, we can use multiple intelligence theory to recognize each child's strengths and provide opportunities for children to use their strengths as well as develop their weak areas in a supportive, nurturing environment.

Verbal-linguistic

People with strong verbal-linguistic intelligence have highly developed verbal skills. They tend to think and express themselves well in words; they use words precisely and enjoy learning new words and new ways to work with words; and they enjoy reading and comprehend well what they read.

Logical-mathematical

People with strong logical-mathematical intelligence are analytical thinkers. They enjoy puzzles and other logic problems, as well as numbers and mathematical formulas; they are attuned to patterns and systems; and they enjoy logical arguments and discussions.

Visual-spatial

People with strong visual-spatial intelligence think in terms of images; they are attuned to anything visual—patterns, colors, shapes—and enjoy expressing what they know and feel in visual ways, such as drawing, painting, and sculpting. They also have a talent for mental visualization.

Musical-rhythmic

People with strong musical-rhythmic intelligence enjoy creating, mimicking, and listening to sounds and rhythms, particularly music. They are sensitive to various sounds, tones, and rhythms, including those found in speech.

Bodily-kinesthetic

People with strong bodily-kinesthetic intelligence enjoy physical movement and perform well in any activity involving lots of body movement, such as dance, drama, sports, and other physical games. They can often learn a physical movement by watching someone else do it.

Intrapersonal

People with strong intrapersonal intelligence are acutely aware of themselves—their feelings, intuitions, thinking processes, and strengths and weaknesses. They work well alone, are usually self-motivated, and often have strong opinions.

Interpersonal

People with strong interpersonal intelligence work well with other people. They often learn better in partnerships or groups and are sensitive and open to other people's perspectives, feelings, and ideas.

Naturalist

People with strong naturalist intelligence have a keen understanding of nature and natural processes and systems. They are excellent observers and classifiers, particularly in the natural world.

Worksheets for Activities

Name: _____

Information Chart

Tribe:	Tribe:
Locations:	Locations:
Traditional housing:	Traditional housing:
Traditional clothing:	Traditional clothing:
Population (then/now):	Population (then/now):
How they lived in the past (food, work, play, transportation):	How they lived in the past (food, work, play, transportation):
Beliefs and traditions:	Beliefs and traditions:
Other interesting information:	Other interesting information:

Educating the Heart, ©2002 Zephyr Press, Tucson, Arizona • 800-232-2187 • www.zephyrpress.com

Name: _____

My mood today is like the color _____

because _____

_____

_____

_____

_____

Name: _____

I like the feel of _____

because _____

Educating the Heart, ©2002 Zephyr Press, Tucson, Arizona • 800-232-2187 • www.zephyrpress.com

Name: _____

The taste of _____

makes me feel _____

because _____

_____

_____

_____

_____

Name: _____

I like the sound of _____

because _____

_____

_____

_____

_____

Educating the Heart, ©2002 Zephyr Press, Tucson, Arizona • 800-232-2187 • www.zephyrpress.com

Name: _____

The smell of _____

makes me remember _____

because _____

Name: _____

I hope _____

Educating the Heart, ©2002 Zephyr Press, Tucson, Arizona • 800-232-2187 • www.zephyrpress.com

Observing Multiple Intelligences

Name: _____

Character/Person: _____

MI: _____

MI: _____

★★★★★★★★★★★★★★★★★★★★★★★★★★★★★★★★★★★★★★

Character/Person: _____

MI: _____

MI: _____

★★★★★★★★★★★★★★★★★★★★★★★★★★★★★★★★★★★★★★

Character/Person: _____

MI: _____

MI: _____

★★★★★★★★★★★★★★★★★★★★★★★★★★★★★★★★★★★★★★

Character/Person: _____

MI: _____

MI: _____

My Multiple Intelligences

Name: _____

Body Movement — Body Smart

Knowing Yourself — Self Smart — ME

Working with Others — People Smart

Naturalist — Nature Smart

Using Music — Music Smart

Understanding by Seeing — Picture Smart

Using Words — Word Smart

Using numbers being Logical — Number Smart — 2 + 1 a

x/÷ abc

Name of Family Member _____

Color each section in the above wheel to show strengths: darker for the stronger areas; lighter for weaker areas. (Or you can color code: blue = very strong; red = medium strong, yellow = weak).

Educating the Heart, ©2002 Zephyr Press, Tucson, Arizona • 800-232-2187 • www.zephyrpress.com

Appendix C

Resources and References

This appendix includes Activity Resources, a section of recommended resources for particular activities; Resources by Category, a section that includes additional book, music, and video recommendations that apply to more than one activity, organized in the following categories—birth and death, cultures (which includes a general celebrations and traditions section, a Native Americans section, and a spirituality and creation stories section), mood music, nature/environment, and values; Teacher Resources, a section of recommended reading for teachers who want to learn more about teaching to the spirit; and References, a section of the titles I consulted while researching and writing this book.

Activity Resources

(Activities are listed in alphabetical order. Activites with no recommended resources are not included.)

All about Me

Martin, Bill, Jr., and Eric Carle. 1997. *Polar Bear, Polar Bear, What Do You Hear?* New York: Henry Holt & Company.

Martin, Bill, Jr., John Archambault, and James Endicott. 1988. *Listen to the Rain*. New York: Henry Holt & Company.

O'Neill, Mary, and John Wallner. 1989. *Hailstones and Halibut Bones*. New York: Doubleday.

Ryan, Pam M. 2001. *Hello, Ocean!* Watertown, Mass.: Charlesbridge Publishing.

Seuss, Dr. 1996. *Mr. Brown Can Moo, Can You?: Dr. Seuss's Book of Wonderful Noises*. New York: Random House.

Seuss, Dr., Steve Johnson, and Lou Fancher. 1996. *My Many Colored Days*. New York: Knopf.

Stepanek, Mattie J. T. 2002. *Hope through Heartsongs*. New York: Hyperion.

Wells, Rosemary. 1994. *Night Sounds, Morning Colors*. New York: Dial Books for Young Readers.

America's First People

(See also the Native Americans section on page 140.)

500 Nations. 1995. Warner Home Video. [series of eight videocassettes: rated NR]

How the West Was Lost, Part 1. 1998. Discovery Communication. [series of three videocassettes: rated NR]

How the West Was Lost, Part 2. 1998. Discovery Communication. [series of four videocassettes: rated NR]

Buddy Reading

Any books the children choose will work, but following are two great titles to recommend to your students. See also any of the titles listed in the Resources by Category section, on pages 140–42.

Anderson, Bob. 1999 *Obo*. Charlottesville, Va.: Hampton Roads Publishing.

Curtis, Chara M, and Cynthia Aldrich. 1994. *All I See Is Part of Me*. Bellevue, Wash.: Illumination Arts.

Character

(See also the Values section on page 142.)

Angels in the Outfield. 1997. [videocassette: rated PG] (pride, self-respect)

A Bug's Life. 2000. Disney/Pixar. [videocassette: rated G] (courage, respect)

Carlson, Nancy L. 1988. *I Like Me!* New York: Viking Kestrel. (self respect)

Collins, Elizabeth H, and Judy Kuusisto. 2001. *The Doll Lady*. Bellevue, Wash.: Illumination Arts. (respect)

Evans, Richard Paul, and Jonathan Linton. 2001. *Tower*. New York: Simon & Schuster. (generosity)

A Far Off Place. 1997. Disney Studios. [videocassette: rated PG] (courage)

Fern Gully: The Last Rainforest. 1992, Twentieth Century Fox. [videocassette: rated G] (respect for nature)

Greenwood, Lee. 1994. "God Bless the U.S.A." *God Bless the U.S.A.* MCA Special Products. (pride)

Henry, O. 1997. *The Gift of the Magi*. New York: Aladdin Paperbacks. (generosity)

Hopkins, Susan, and Jeffry Winters, eds. 1990. *Discover the World: Empowering Children to Value Themselves, Others and the Earth*. Gabriola Island, B.C.: New Society Publishers. (respect)

HumanityQuest.com. "Generosity." www.humanityquest.com/topic/Index.asp?theme1=generosity. Accessed February 28, 2002.

Jimenez, Francisco, and Claire Cotts. 2000. *The Christmas Gift*. Boston, Mass.: Houghton Mifflin. (generosity)

Kelly, R. 1996. "I Believe I Can Fly." *I Believe I Can Fly.* Jive Records. (pride)

Lawson, Julie. 1996. *Cougar Cove.* Victoria, B.C.: Orca Book Publishers. (courage)

Lindquist, Susan Hart. 1999. *Summer Soldiers.* New York: Delacorte Press. (courage)

Melmed, Laura Krauss. 2000. *Moishe's Miracle: A Hanukkah Story.* New York: Harpercollins. (generosity)

Millman, Dan. 1991. *Secret of the Peaceful Warrior.* Tiburon, Calif.: H.J. Kramer Inc. (courage)

Mr. Holland's Opus. 1997. Hollywood Pictures. [videocassette: rated PG] (generosity, pride)

Paulsen, G. 1990. *Woodsong.* New York: Bradbury Press. (respect for nature)

Peet, Bill. 1984. *Cowardly Clyde.* Reprint edition. Boston, Mass.: Houghton Mifflin. (courage)

Pellegrino, Marjorie White, and John Lund. 2000. *My Grandma's the Mayor: A Story for Children about Community Spirit and Pride.* Washington D.C.: Magination Press. (pride)

Remember the Titans. 2001. Disney Studios. [videocassette: rated PG] (courage)

Rudy. 1997. Columbia/Tristar Studios. [videocassette: rated PG] (earning respect, courage)

Senshu, Noriko. 2000. *Sonny's Dream.* Charlottesville, Va.: Hampton Roads Publishing. (courage)

Seuss, Dr. 1998. *The Big Brag.* New York: Random House. (pride)

Shrek. 2001. Dreamworks. [videocassette: rated PG] (self-respect, courage)

Silverstein, Shel. 1999. *The Giving Tree.* New York: Harpercollins. (generosity)

Star Wars series. 1997. Twentieth Century Fox. [videocassette: rated PG] (courage)

Testa, Maria. 2001. *Some Kind of Pride.* New York: Delacorte. (pride)

U2. 1988. "Pride (In the Name of Love)." *Rattle and Hum.* Island Records.

Clan Animal

Maclean, Charles, and David McAllister. 1997. *Clans and Tartans.* Gretna, La.: Pelican Publishing.

McNutt, Nan. 1997. *The Button Blanket: A Northwest Coast Indian Art Activity Book.* Seattle, Wash.: Sasquatch Books.

Michal, Kelly, and Patricia Lou. 2000. *The Stump Fairies of Miller Hill.* Bloomington, Ind.: 1st Books Library.

Reed, Marcelina. 1996. *Seven Clans of the Cherokee Society.* Cherokee, N.C.: Cherokee Publishing.

Stinnett, Leia. 1998. *Animal Tales: Spiritual Lessons from Our Animal Friends.* Flagstaff, Ariz.: Light Technology Publications.

Creation Stories

See the Spirituality and Creation Stories section on page 141.

Drinking Flower

Cole, Joanna. 1995. *The Magic School Bus Plants Seeds: A Book about How Living Things Grow.* New York: Scholastic Trade.

Taylor, Helen. 1998. *Plants Feed on Sunlight: And Other Facts about Things That Grow.* Brookfield, Conn.: Copper Beech Books.

Flower Sets

Billstein, Rick, Shlomo Libeskind, and Johnny W. Lott. 2000. *A Problem Solving Approach to Mathematics for Elementary School Teachers.* Reading, Mass.: Addison-Wesley Publishing.

Future Places

Gifford, Clive. 1999. *How the Future Began: Machines.* New York: Kingfisher.

———. 2000. *How the Future Began: Everyday Life.* New York: Kingfisher.

Jetsons: First Episodes. 1991. Turner Home Entertainment. [videocassette: rated NR]

Jetsons: The Movie. 1993. Universal Studios. [videocassette: rated G]

Star Trek (any of the many movies and television series, but note the different ratings)

Wilson, Anthony. 1999. *How the Future Began: Communications.* New York: Kingfisher.

Giving a Million

Barry, David. 1994. *The Rajah's Rice: A Mathematical Folktale from India.* New York: W.H. Freeman and Company.

Ryan, Pam M. 1994. *One Hundred Is a Family.* New York: Hyperion Books for Children.

Schwartz, David. 1989. *If You Made a Million*. New York: Lothrop, Lee & Shepard.

———. 1993. *How Much is a Million?* New York: Mulberry Books.

I Would Be Good

Morissette, Alanis. 1998. "That I Would Be Good." *Supposed Former Infatuation Junkie*. Maverick Recording Company. [sound recording]—*or*

Morissette, Alanis. 1999. "That I Would Be Good." *Alanis Morissette: MTV Unplugged*. Maverick Recording Company. [sound recording]

Kindness Tree

Gruelle, Johnny. 1999. *Raggedy Ann's Candy Heart Wisdom: Words of Love and Friendship*. New York: Simon & Schuster.

Moncure, Jane Belk. 1997. *The Child's World of Kindness*. Plymouth, Minn.: Child's World.

Rice, David L. 1999. *Because Brian Hugged His Mother*. Nevada City, Calif.: Dawn Publishing.

Knowing Myself

Bown, Deni. 1991. *The Visual Dictionary of the Human Body*. New York: DK Publishing.

Cooper, Kenneth H. 1985. *The Aerobics Program for Total Well-Being: Exercise, Diet, Emotional Balance*. Reissue edition. New York: Bantam Doubleday Dell.

Delafosse, Claude. 2000. *Human Body: Hidden World*. New York: Scholastic Trade.

Levchuck, Caroline M., Michele I. Drohan, Jane Kelly Kosek, Sharon Rose, and Neil Schlager. 2000. *Healthy Living: Exercise, Nutrition and Other Healthy Habits*. Detroit, Mich.: UXL.

Life Circle

Little, Elbert Luther & Elbert Luther Little, Jr. 1980. *The National Audubon Society Field Guide to North American Trees: Eastern Region*. New York: Knopf.

Little, Elbert Luther, Jr. 1980. *The National Audubon Society Field Guide to North American Trees: Western Region*. New York: Knopf.

Milne, Lorus J. 1980. *National Audubon Society Field Guide to North American Insects and Spiders*. New York: Knopf.

O'Toole, Christopher, ed. 1995. *The Encyclopedia of Insects*. New York: Checkmark Books.

Math in Nature

Brookes, Mona. 1995. *Drawing with Children: A Creative Method for Adult Beginners, Too*. New York: Putnam.

Wise Brown, Margaret. 1999. *The Important Book*. New York: Harpercollins Children's Books.

Media Awareness

Looney Tunes: Chariots of Fur. 1996. Warner Bros. [videocassette]

The Three Stooges. 1998. TV Classics Collection, Madacy Entertainment. [videocassette]

Multiple Intelligences

(See also the suggestions in the Values section, on page 142.)

Demi. 1990. *The Empty Pot*. New York: Henry Holt and Company.

Prechtel, Martín. 2001. *The Disobedience of the Daughter of the Sun: Ecstasy and Time*. Cambridge, Mass.: Yellow Moon.

Rowling, J. K. 1998 *Harry Potter and the Sorceror's Stone*. New York: A.A. Levine Books.

———. 1999. *Harry Potter and the Chamber of Secrets*. New York: A.A. Levine Books.

———. 1999. *Harry Potter and the Prisoner of Azkaban*. New York: A.A. Levine Books.

———. 2000. *Harry Potter and the Goblet of Fire*. New York: A.A. Levine Books.

Rugrats (any Rugrats cartoon, television or movie, contains characters showing multiple intelligences)

Sanderson, Ruth. 1997. *Rose Red and Snow White: A Grimms Fairy Tale*. New York: Little Brown & Co.

Star Trek: The Next Generation (any of the television shows or movies)

Passionate Questions

Hoban, Tana. 1999. *I Wonder*. San Diego, Calif.: Harcourt Brace.

Stock, Gregory. 1988. *The Kids' Book of Questions*. New York: Workman Publishing Company.

Wollard, Kathy. 1993. *How Come?* New York: Workman Publishing Company.

Pen Pals

Europa Pages. "International Pen Friends for Schools, Colleges, and Universities." 1997–2001. www.europa-pages.com/school_form.html. Accessed March 15, 2002.

Planet Britain. "General: Penpals." http://www.brithighcomm.org.nz/general/penpals.html. Accessed March 15, 2002.

www.link. "Penpals." fp.uni.edu/ljohnson/www.htm. Accessed March 15, 2002. (Scroll down to "Penpals" and click on either culture box or e-mail penpals.)

Physical Education (in general)

Hendricks, Gay, and Thomas B. Roberts. 1977. *The Second Centering Book: More Awareness Activities for Children and Adults to Relax the Body and Mind*. New York: Prentice Hall Press.

Khalsa, Shakta Kaur. 1998. *Fly Like a Butterfly: Yoga for Children*. Portland, Ore.: Rudra Press.

Stewart, Mary, and Kathy Phillips. 1992. *Yoga for Children*. New York: Simon & Schuster.

Reading and Writing Activities (in general)

Bottner, Barbara, and Peggy Rathman. 1992. *Bootsie Barker Bites*. New York: Putnam.

Hahn, Mary Downing. 1991. *Stepping on the Cracks*. New York: Clarion Books.

Springer, Melissa. 1998. *Important Things*. Birmingham, Ala.: Crane Hill Publishers.

Self-Portraits

Spero, James, ed. 1990. *Old Master Portrait Drawings*. New York: Dover.

Songs from the Heart

10,000 Maniacs. 1992. "These Are Days." *These Are Days*. Elektra Entertainment.

Brooks, Garth. 1992. "We Shall Be Free." *The Chase*. Liberty.

Denver, John. 2001. "Rhymes and Reasons." *An Evening with John Denver*. RCA.

Fogelberg, Dan. 1985. "Higher You Climb." *High Country Snows*. Epic Records.

Loggins, Kenny. 1997. "Conviction of the Heart." *Yesterday, Today, Tomorrow: The Greatest Hits*. Columbia.

Stevens, Cat. 2000. "Peace Train." *The Very Best of Cat Stevens*. A&M Records.

Walker, Clay. 1999. "The Chain of Love." *Live, Laugh, Love*. Giant.

Williams, Vanessa. 1995. "Colors of the Wind." *Colors of the Wind*. Hollywood Records.

Womack, Lee Ann. 2000. *I Hope You Dance*. MCA.

Talking Circle

Baldwin, Christina, and Colleen Kelley. 1998. *Calling the Circle: The First and Future Culture*. New York: Bantam Books.

Jastrab, Joseph. 1991. "Using a Talking Stick." *Wingspan: Journal of Male Spirit*, (April/June).

Pór, George. "The 'Talking Stick' Circle: An Ancient Tool for Better Decision Making and Strengthening Community." January 16, 2000. www.vision-nest.com/btbc/kgarden/tscircle.shtml. Accessed March 15, 2002.

Word Tools

Bottner, Barbara, and Peggy Rathman. 1992. *Bootsie Barker Bites*. New York: Putnam.

Hazen, Barbara Shook, and R. W. Alley. 1997. *The New Dog*. New York: Dial Books for Young Readers.

Kalish, Ginny. 2001. *Rachel Rude Rowdy*. Tucson, Ariz.: Zephyr Press.

Resources by Category

Birth and Death

Barron, T. A. 1990. *Heartlight.* New York: Philomel Books.

Cohen, Cindy Klein. 1997. *Daddy's Promise.* Bloomfield Hills, Mich.: Promise Publications.

Frasier, Debra. 1991. *On the Day You Were Born.* New York: The Trumpet Club.

Mundy, Michaelene. 1998. *Sad isn't Bad: A Good-Grief Guidebook for Kids Dealing with Loss.* St. Meinrad, Ind.: Abbey Press.

Palmer, Pat. 1994. *I Wish I Could Hold Your Hand: A Child's Guide to Grief and Loss.* San Luis Obispo, Calif.: Impact Publishing.

Cultures

Celebrations and Traditions

Brady, April A. 1995. *Kwanzaa Karamu: Cooking and Crafts for a Kwanzaa Feast.* Minneapolis, Minn.: Carolrhoda Books.

Casteneda, Omar, and Enrique Sanchez. 1993. *Abuela's Weave.* New York: Lee & Low Books.

Cha, Dia. 1996. *Dia's Story Cloth.* New York: Lee & Low Books.

Drucker, Malka, and Eve Chwast. 1992. *Grandma's Latkes.* San Diego: Harcourt Brace Jovanovich.

Elmer, Margaret, Charlotte Beall, and Sarah Robertson. 1997. *Festivals of Light: A Hands-on Activity Book.* Seattle, Wash.: The Children's Museum (e-mail: shop@thechildrensmuseum.org to order).

Evans, Richard Paul. 1998. *The Christmas Candle.* New York: Simon & Schuster Books for Young Readers.

Flournoy, Valerie, and Jerry Pinkney. 1985. *The Patchwork Quilt.* New York: Dial Books.

Gibbons, Gail. 1999. *Santa Who?* New York: Morrow Junior Books.

Howard, Ellen, and Ronald Himler. 1996. *The Log Cabin Quilt.* New York: Holiday House.

Hoyt-Goldsmith, DIANE. 1993. *Celebrating Kwanzaa.* New York: Holiday House.

———. 1999. *Las Posadas: An Hispanic Christmas Celebration.* New York: Holiday House.

Jackson, Ellen. 1994. *The Winter Solstice.* Brookfield, Conn.: The Millbrook Press.

Lasky, Kathryn. 1994. *Days of the Dead.* New York: Hyperion Books for Children.

Lee & Low Books: Multicultural Literature for Children. 1997–2002. www.leeandlow.com. Accessed March 15, 2002.

Pandya, Mennal. 1994. *Here Comes Diwali.* Wellesley, Mass.: MeeRa Publications.

Pennington, Daniel, and Don Stewart. 1994. *Itse Sel: Cherokee Harvest Festival.* Watertown, Mass.: Charlesbridge Publishing.

Pinkney, Andrea Davis. 1993. *Seven Candles for Kwanzaa.* New York: Dial Books for Young Readers.

Polacco, Patricia. 1988. *The Keeping Quilt.* New York: Simon & Schuster.

Riverdale School District. "Related Web Sites." February 5, 2002. www.riverdale.k12.or.us/~ktonning/97_98/websites.htm. Accessed March 15, 2002.

Rylant, Cynthia. 1987. *Children of Christmas.* New York: Orchard Books.

Simon, Norma. 1994. *The Story of Hanukkah.* New York: Harpercollins Publishers.

Sun, Chyng Feng. 1994. *Mama Bear.* Boston, Mass.: Houghton Mifflin Company.

Wyeth, Sharon Dennis. 1994. *The World of Daughter McGuire.* New York: Delacorte Press.

Native Americans

Baker, Olaf. 1985. *Where the Buffaloes Begin.* New York: Penguin.

Baylor, Byrd. 1987. *The Desert Is Theirs.* New York: Aladdin Paperbacks.

Bopp, Judie. 1989. *The Sacred Tree: Reflections on Native American Spirituality.* Wilmot, Wisc.: Lotus Light Publications.

Caduto, Michael J., and Joseph Bruchac. 1994. *Keepers of the Night: Native American Stories and Nocturnal Activities for Children.* Golden, Colo.: Fulcrum Publishing.

George, Jean Craighead. 1987. *The Talking Earth.* New York: Harpercollins Children's Books.

Goble, Paul. 1984. *Buffalo Woman.* New York: Simon & Schuster.

Miles, Miska. 1985. *Annie and the Old One.* New York: Little Brown & Co.

NativeTech: Native American Technology and Art. 1994–2002. www.nativetech.org. Accessed March 15, 2002.

Native Web: Resources for Indigenous Cultures around the World. 1994–2002. www.nativeweb.org. Accessed March 15, 2002.

Nerburn, Kent, ed. 2001. *The Soul of An Indian: And Other Writings from Ohiyesa (Charles Alexander Eastman).* Novato, Calif.: New World Library.

Seattle, Chief 1991. *Brother Eagle, Sister Sky.* New York: Dial Books.

Swamp, Chief Jake 1995. *Giving Thanks: A Native American Good Morning Message.* New York: Lee & Low Books.

Yolen, Jane. 1992. *Encounter.* New York: Harcourt Brace Jovanovich.

Spirituality and Creation Stories

Anderson, Bob. 1999 *Obo.* Charlottesville, Va.: Hampton Roads Publishing.

Berry, James. 1997. *First Palm Trees: An Anancy Spiderman Story.* New York: Simon & Schuster.

Bierhorst, John. 1993. *The Woman Who Fell from the Sky: The Iroquois Story of Creation.* New York: William Morrow & Company, Inc.

Curtis, Chara M, and Cynthia Aldrich. 1994. *All I See Is Part of Me.* Bellevue, Wash.: Illumination Arts.

Elkins, David N. 1998. *Beyond Religion: A Personal Program for Building a Spiritual Life Outside the Walls of Traditional Religion.* Wheaton, Ill.: Theosophical Publishing House.

Gellman, Marc, and Thomas Hartman. 1995. *How Do You Spell God? Answers to the Big Questions from Around the World.* New York: William Morrow & Company.

Hampton Roads Publishing for the Evolving Human Spirit. www.hrpub.com. Accessed March 15, 2002.

Hausman, Gerald. 1999. *The Coyote Bead.* Charlottesville, Va.: Hampton Roads Publishing.

Hickman, Martha Whitmore. 1993. *And God Created Squash: How the World Began.* Morton Grove, Ill.: Albert Whitman & Company.

Hill, Franklin. 2000. *Wings of Change.* Bellevue, Wash.: Illuminations Arts.

Internet School Library Media Center. "Moral Values and Spirituality in Children's and Young Adult Literature." falcon.jmu.edu/~ramseyil/moral.htm. Accessed March 15, 2002.

Jenkins, Peggy Davison. 1995. *Nurturing Spirituality in Children: Simple Hands-on Activities.* Hillsboro, Ore.: Beyond Words Publishing.

Kornfield, Jack. 1994. *Buddha's Little Instruction Book.* New York: Bantam Books.

Lester, Julius. 1999. *When the Beginning Began: Stories about God, the Creatures, and Us.* San Diego: Harcourt Brace.

McCarley, Becky. 1999. *Herman's Magical Universe.* Charlottesville, Va.: Hampton Roads Publishing.

Ontario Consultants on Religious Tolerance. www.religioustolerance.org. Accessed March 15, 2002.

Roberts, Jane. 2000. *Emir's Education in the Proper Use of Magical Powers.* Charlottesville, Va.: Hampton Roads Publishing.

Rohmer, Harriet, and Mary Anchondo. 1988. *How We Came to the Fifth World: A Creation Story from Ancient Mexico.* San Francisco, Calif.: Children's Book Press.

Spirituality and Consciousness: Books for Children of All Ages. 1998–2001. www.4light.com/childrens.html. Accessed March 15, 2002.

Walsch, Neale Donald. 1995. *Conversations with God: An Uncommon Dialogue.* New York: G.P. Putnam's Sons.

———.1998. *The Little Soul and the Sun.* Charlottesville, Va.: Hampton Roads Publishing.

Williams, Sheron. 1992. *And in the Beginning.* New York: Atheneum Publishers.

Wood, Douglas. 1992. *Old Turtle.* Duluth, Minn.: Pfeifer-Hamilton Publishers.

Mood Music

Enya. *Shepard Moons* by Kenny G. 1992. *Breathless.* Arista Records.

Lifescapes Series (from Target): *Relaxing Piano, Scottish Moors, Garden Rain, Mexico.*

Williams, John. 1995. *Schindler's List: The Classic Film Music of John Williams.* Silva America.

Yanni. 1993. *In My Time.* Private.

Nature/Environment

Atkins, Jeannine, and Venantius Pinto. 2000. *Aani and the Tree Huggers.* New York: Lee & Low Books.

Bruchac, Joseph. 1995. *Native Plant Stories,* from Keepers of Life series, by Michael J. Caduto. Golden, Colo.: Fulcrum Publishing.

Carrier, Lark. 1996. *A Tree's Tale.* New York: Dial Books for Young Readers.

Cornell, Joseph. 1987. *Listening to Nature: How to Deepen Your Awareness of Nature.* Nevada City, Calif.: Dawn Publications.

Values

Ada, Alma Flor. 1996. *Jordi's Star.* New York: Putnam.

Andersen, Hans Christian. 1993. *The Ugly Duckling.* St. Petersburg, Fla.: Worthington Press.

Baylor, Byrd. 1994. *The Table Where Rich People Sit.* New York: Simon & Schuster.

Demi. 1990. *The Empty Pot.* New York: Henry Holt and Company.

Faulkner, William J. 1995. *Brer Tiger and the Big Wind.* New York: Morrow Junior Books.

Heidel, John, and Marion Lyman-Mersereau. 1999. *Character Education.* Nashville, Tenn.: Incentive Publications.

Scholes, Katherine. 1994. *Peace Begins with You.* Boston: Little, Brown, and Company.

Teacher Resources

Baloche, Lynda A. 1997. *Cooperative Classroom: The Empowering Learning.* New York: Prentice Hall.

Brooks, Jacqueline Grennon, and Martin G. Brooks. 1999. *In Search of Understanding: The Case for Constructivist Classrooms.* Alexandria, Va.: Association for Supervision and Curriculum Development.

Campbell, Linda, Bruce Campbell, and Dee Dickinson. 1999. *Teaching and Learning through Multiple Intelligences.* Boston: Allyn and Bacon

Carol Hurst's Children's Literature Site. 1999. www.carolhurst.com. Accessed March 15, 2002.

Childre, Doc Lew. 1996. *Teaching Children to Love: 80 Games and Fun Activities for Raising Balanced Children in Unbalanced Times.* Boulder Creek, Calif.: Planetary Publications.

Choquette, Sonia. 1999. *The Wise Child: A Spiritual Guide to Nurturing Your Child's Intuition.* New York: Three Rivers Press.

Daleo, Morgan Simone, and Frank Riccio. 1996. *Curriculum of Love: Cultivating the Spiritual Nature of Children.* Charlottesville, Va.: Grace Publishing and Communications.

Dyer, Wayne W. 1993. *Everyday Wisdom.* Carson, Calif.: Hay House, Inc.

Galyean, Beverly. 1983. *Mind Sight: Learning through Imaging.* Long Beach, Calif.: Center for Integrative Learning.

Gardner, Howard. 2000. *Intelligence Reframed: Multiple Intelligences for the 21st Century.* Boulder, Colo.: Basic Books.

Glazer, Steven, ed. 1999. *The Heart of Learning: Spirituality in Education.* Los Angeles: J.P. Tarcher.

Herschfelder, Arlene. 1986. *Happily May I Walk.* New York: Scribners.

Hill, Bonnie Campbell, and Cynthia A. Ruptic. 1994. *Practical Aspects of Authentic Assessment: Putting the Pieces Together.* Norwood, Mass.: Christopher-Gordon Publishing.

Marlowe, Bruce A., and Marilyn L. Page. 1998. *Creating and Sustaining the Constructivist Classroom.* Thousand Oaks, Calif.: Corwin Publishing.

Montgomery, Kathleen. 2000. *Authentic Assessment: A Guide for Elementary Teachers.* New York: Longman.

Nelsen, Jane. 1996. *Positive Discipline.* New York: Ballantine Books.

Nixon, Susan. "Six Traits Writing Assessment." June 2001. 6traits.cyberspaces.net. Accessed March 15, 2002.

Northwest Regional Educational Laboratory. "Scoring 6+1 Trait™ Writing." March 14, 2002. www.nwrel.org/assessment/definitions.asp?d=1. Accessed March 15, 2002.

Slavin, Robert E. 1994. *Cooperative Learning: Theory, Research, and Practice.* Boston: Allyn & Bacon.

Spandel, Vicki. 2000. *Creating Writers through 6-Trait Writing Assessment and Instruction.* New York: Longman.

Springer, Melissa. 1997. *Important Things.* Birmingham, Ala.: Crane Hill Publishers.

Teachers@Random. "Thematic Index." www.randomhouse.com/teachers/guides/trc_thematic.html. Accessed March 15, 2002.

Tombari, Martin L., and Gary D. Borich. 1998. *Authentic Assessment in the Classroom: Applications and Practice.* New York: Prentice Hall

Wahl, Mark. 1999. *Math for Humans: Teaching through the 8 Intelligences.* Fairfield, Conn.: JMC Pub. Services.

References

Anonymous 2000. "New Church-School Guidelines." *The Christian Century* 117: 10.

Bender, James Frederick. 1994. *How to Talk Well.* New York: McGraw-Hill.

Benson, Herbert, and George H. Gallup International Institute. 1996. "Religious Preference—National." www.prrc.com/data.html. Accessed February 26, 2000.

Blue Mountain Arts. 1999. *The Language of Teaching: Thoughts on the Art of Teaching and the Meaning of Education.* Boulder, Colo.: Blue Mountain Press.

Dyer, Wayne. 1993. *Everyday Wisdom.* Carson, Calif.: Hay House.

Edwards, June. 1998. "The Debate Over Humanism and Democracy." *Opposing Censorship in the Public Schools*: 14–24. Mahwah, N.J.: Lawrence Erlbaum Associates.

Eisler, Riane. 1998. "Spiritual Courage." *Tikkun* 14: 15–20.

Elkins, David N. 1998. *Beyond Religion: A Personal Program for Building a Spiritual Life Outside the Walls of Traditional Religion.* Wheaton, Ill.: Theosophical Publishing House.

Ely, Virginia. 1947. *I Quote: A Collection of Ancient and Modern Wisdom and Inspiration.* Westwood, N.J.: Fleming H. Revell.

Feeney, D. J. 1996. "Purposeful Self: Accessing Sensory Motifs as Empowerment in Flow States and Clinical Interventions." *The Journal of Humanistic Psychology* 36:94–116.

Foxworth, Marlin. 1998. "Putting spirituality in public schools." *Tikkun* 13: 51–54.

Gilbran, Kahlil. 1983. *The Prophet.* New York: Alfred A. Knopf.

Hart, Tobin. 1998. "Inspiration: Exploring the Experience and Its Meaning." *The Journal of Humanistic Psychology* 38:7–38.

Iannone, Ronald V., and Patricia A. Obenauf. 1999. "Toward Spirituality in Curriculum and Teaching." *Education* 119:737–745.

Johnson, Aostre N. 1999. "A Postmodern Perspective on Education and Spirituality: Hearing Many Voices." *Encounter: Education for Meaning and Social Justice* 12:41–48.

Kessler, Rachael. 2000. *The Soul of Education: Helping Students Find Connection, Compassion, and Character at School.* Alexandria, Va.: Association for Supervision and Curriculum Development.

Kornfield, Jack. 1994. *Buddha's Little Instruction Book.* New York: Bantam Books.

Kramnick, Isaac, and R. Laurence Moore. 1999. "Religion in Our Schools: Teach Values, Not Religion." *The World & I* 14:41, 45.

Lantieri, Linda, ed. 2001. *Schools with Spirit: Nurturing the Inner Lives of Children and Teachers.* Boston: Beacon Press.

Lear, Norman. 1991. "Education for the Human Spirit." *The Education Digest* 6:33–35.

Mandino, Og. 1983. *The Greatest Salesman in the World.* New York: Bantam Books.

Maslow, Abraham H. 1971. *The Farther Reaches of Human Nature.* New York: The Viking Press.

Miller, Ron. 1999. "Education and the Evolution of the Cosmos." *Encounter: Education for Meaning and Social Justice* 12:21–28.

———. 2000. "Holistic Education and the Emerging Culture." *Spirituality in Education OnLine.* csf.colorado.edu/sine/transcripts/miller.html. Accessed January 25, 2000.

Morissette, Alanis. 1998. "That I Would Be Good." *Supposed Former Infatuation Junkie.* Maverick Recording Company. [sound recording]

Myers, Barbara, and Michael Myers. 1999. "Engaging Children's Spirit and Spirituality through Literature." *Childhood Education* 76:28–32.

Neil, William. 1974. *Concise Dictionary of Religious Quotations.* Grand Rapids, Mich.: William B. Eardmans Publishing Company.

Palmer, Parker J. 1999. "Evoking the Spirit." *Educational Leadership* 56:6–11.

Running Press. 1994. *Faith, Hope, and Love: An Inspirational Treasury of Quotations.* Philadelphia, Pa.: Running Press.

Tripp, Rhoda Thomas. 1970. *The International Thesaurus of Quotations.* New York: Thomas Y. Crowell Company.

Walsch, Neale Donald. 1995. *Conversations with God: An Uncommon Dialogue.* New York: Putnam.

Wilber, Ken. 1998. "The Integral Vision: The Good, the True, and the Beautiful." In *The Eye of Spirit*, 1–36. Boston and London: Shambhala.

Woolfolk, Anita. 2000. *Educational Psychology.* Boston: Allyn & Bacon.

Index _____

About the Author

Alison Hagee came to education as a second career. Her first degree is a B.S. in aerospace engineering from Boston University. After 10 years in the environmental testing and consulting field, Alison longed for a career that was more fulfilling and hands on. She made the switch to education and graduated with an M.A. The content of this book formed the basis of her dissertation.

Alison has enjoyed the challenge of teaching in kindergarten through eighth-grade classrooms. She has recently undertaken her most important teaching role with the birth of her first child. She lives with her husband, Eric, and her daughter, Celeste, in Seattle.